PRAISE FOR TEACH FOR I...

'I truly believe that what Teach For-I... ...
revolutionary, very positive, and will ... ay
our nation mo... forward in the years ... ...ing
like this was around when I was passing ou... ...llege.'
Aamir Khan, Actor

'Teach For India is like Shakespeare's "gentle rain from heaven" — it blesseth him that gives and him that takes. It is becoming a force for driving positive change in this country as it impacts futures and changes lives. The Teach for India story needs to be told and I believe this book is an important step in spreading its message.'
Anand Mahindra, Chairman and MD, Mahindra Group

'Teach For India is doing an amazing job of helping even the odds for thousands of children. It has brought together young men and women who want to make a difference, and what better way to make a difference than through children? The Teach For India story is about moulding lives and shaping futures.' **Jaideep Bose, Chief Editor, *Times of India***

'Teach For India has the potential to have a possibly greater impact in catalyzing and developing a movement to provide all of India's children with the opportunities they deserve.' **Wendy Kopp, CEO and Co-Founder, Teach For All**

'Teach for India teaches India's best and brightest compassion, perseverance, emotional resilience, and the value of constantly thinking on your feet — the core values needed for success in endeavours after. It will also give you love and oceans of gratitude from the children you teach and from their families. What more can one ask for from the Universe?' **Rahul Bose, Actor, Social Activist**

'Without a doubt, Teach for India is national service. It's incredible how real the change is that Fellows have brought to education.'
Arnab Goswami, News Anchor, *Times Now*

'Teach for India Fellowship is not just about being a teacher for a couple of years, but teaching yourself invaluable lessons for life.'
Chetan Bhagat, Author

'When I grow up, I am going to join Teach For India. I will be there until I am 30. After that I will try and join the Indian Embassy. If I fail, I will try again. If I fail a second time, I will try again. If I fail after that I will just stay in Teach For India for my whole life.' **Khalil Mulla, Teach For India student**

REDRAWING
INDIA

REDRAWING INDIA

THE TEACHFORINDIA STORY

KOVID GUPTA   SHAHEEN MISTRI

Dear Dutta,

Thankyou for all the guidance!

sincerely,
Kovid

RANDOM HOUSE INDIA

Published by Random House India in 2014
1

Copyright © Kovid Gupta and Shaheen Mistri 2014

Random House Publishers India Pvt Ltd
7th Floor, Infinity Tower C, DLF Cyber City
Gurgaon – 122002
Haryana

Random House Group Limited
20 Vauxhall Bridge Road
London SW1V 2SA
United Kingdom

978 81 8400 563 9

This book is sold subject to the condition that it shall not,
by way of trade or otherwise, be lent, resold, hired out, or
otherwise circulated without the publisher's prior consent in any
form of binding or cover other than that in which it is published
and without a similar condition including this condition being
imposed on the subsequent purchaser.

Photographs © Sunhil Sippy

Typeset in Electra LT by R. Ajith Kumar

Printed and bound in India by Replika Press Private Limited

A PENGUIN RANDOM HOUSE COMPANY

*To every child in India,
and their potential to shape India's future*

CONTENTS

Foreword by Anu Aga — xi
Preface and Acknowledgements — xvii

1. Didi — 1
2. We Will Rise — 17
3. A Moral Imperative — 47
4. Teach for India is Inevitable — 65
5. Firki — 79
6. The Niners — 97
7. The First Year — 111
8. This is Real — 137
9. The Colours of a Movement — 163
10. Seva — 186
11. The Path So Far — 209
12. Find Your Light — 231

Afterword — 250
References — 257
A Note on the Authors — 260

FOREWORD

When Shaheen asked me to write a preface to this book, I was delighted. It gave me a chance to reflect on my seven-year long association with Teach For India, right from its inception to the admirable position it occupies today.

It was in the late 1990s that I met Shaheen. Though a social worker by training, destiny took me to the corporate world. I had been involved in some form of social work but never in a planned, systematic way. My son, who passed away in a car accident, had always wanted a part of our earnings to go towards social causes. After his death, I was looking for a credible NGO to work with and many people suggested I meet Shaheen, who ran Akanksha at the time. Armed with several questions, I met her in Mumbai and was fascinated by her and her passion for the cause of education. It is through Shaheen and Akanksha that I came to know about the educational landscape of India and realized the urgent need for change.

I will share my personal experience with a girl named Seema Kamble who lived in a Mumbai slum. She attended an Akanksha centre and thanks to the influence of her teachers and her own determination, she graduated from high school and then got her undergraduate degree. She went on to apply to the competitive Teach For India Fellowship where only 5-7 percent of the applicants are chosen, and she was one of the selected candidates. After completing her two-year Fellowship, today, she is the Principal of the 3.2.1 School, a school for low-income students run in partnership with the government.

I have again seen with my own eyes the power of education. My friend, Dr Mashelkar, who was the head of the Council of Scientific and Industrial Research (CSIR), came from an economically disadvantaged background. His father had died when he was six. But fortunately for him, his almost illiterate mother pushed him to continue his studies. He went to a municipal school in Mumbai and eventually went on to finish his Ph.D. We know the rest of the story.

Seven years ago, Shaheen excitedly told me about Teach For America, which had brought about systemic change in the US educational system. She wanted to try out this idea in India and asked if I would be her partner. Anyone who knows Shaheen would have experienced her magnetic power to get people excited about a venture. We invited Wendy Kopp, the Founder of Teach For America, to India and worked with McKinsey to develop a five-year blueprint. I am delighted to say that we have surpassed my expectations.

I greatly admire Teach For India's bold aspiration to provide an excellent education to all children. I believe in its approach to drive systemic change through leaders who are equipped with the values and skills to transform children's lives. I have been into classrooms and seen what our Fellows are able to do. And I have met many of our Alumni and seen their on-going commitment to systemic change.

There is so much in our system that needs to change, for us to reverse our failing public education system. India still faces an acute shortage of 1.2 million teachers—its Teacher Training Institutes are crumbling, as evidenced by a meager 14 percent of teachers passing the Teacher Eligibility Test (TET), and training of school principals is virtually unheard of.

Unfortunately, with tragic consequences, the profession of teaching has lost its sheen. It is not an aspirational profession in India. If a surgeon does not do his job well, word will go around and patients will quickly stop coming. This is the same for a lawyer or any other professional; but if a teacher spends all her life without impacting her students, nobody stops her from being a teacher. Where we need the highest quality and the greatest accountability, we are willing to live with mediocrity. It is time we imagine and create an India where teaching becomes aspirational; where the profession attracts the best of talent, is respected, and our teachers meet the highest expectations.

Teach For India does two things—one, it places excellent teachers for two years in classrooms with students who need them the most and two, it creates an Alumni movement where people like Seema go on to make a lifetime commitment to education, and others impact education from diverse sectors like politics, technology, and business. I have seen the two years alter students in a way they probably never imagined.

In a short span of five years, Teach For India already has 930 teachers teaching across 6 cities. To me, it is incredible that Teach For India has created a platform where this year alone 13,000 passionate, well-educated graduates from some of the best colleges and companies in the country competed for just 500 seats in order to teach, and after that, to be a leader working for educational equity.

The seeds of inspiration that are spreading through our 30,000 students and their families, our 900 Fellows, 700 alumni and their networks, seem to me the beginning of a revolution that will lead India to a better tomorrow.

We know for sure that when we educate a child well, we improve her ability to make choices and lead a healthy and productive life. So, in the myriad challenges that our nation faces, I believe that giving every child a good education will be the single most effective instrument to bring about fundamental change for an India that we wish to create—an India that lives up to its Constitutional promise.

Two hundred million children in this country are waiting to attain the excellent education they deserve. It is a daunting challenge. I believe that more than any other time in our history, we have the resources, ideas, and skills to solve a problem of this magnitude now. The question is do we have the will? Are we willing to join hands and work together—irrespective of the sector we come from or the diversity of our backgrounds? More importantly, are we bold enough to dream beyond the realities of today? Are we bold enough to dream of the India we all wish it to be?

Teach For India has envisioned such a dream, a courageous dream—to reimagine and create a vibrant India. In this dream, we see every child in India with access to an excellent education. Let us prove that we are a nation capable of realizing this dream and have the will and fortitude to get there. I invite everyone reading this to join this movement to make this dream a reality and to get India to a place where truly, like the title of this book says, it is Redrawn. Each of you can contribute in your way, directly by teaching, or indirectly by contributing resources or by advocating for educational equity. I turn to the generosity of each of you to help this wonderful cause and take India to new heights.

Anu Aga
August, 2014

PREFACE AND ACKNOWLEDGEMENTS

I could have written a book this size filled with just the names of all the people who have brought Teach For India to this place. I have the deepest gratitude for:

The children of India, who give me the privilege of doing this work each day.

The families of our children, who want in their hearts for their children's lives to be better than those they lead; kinder, easier, more meaningful.

Our Fellows and Alumni, men and women who see beyond today to tomorrow, and who take the tiny, difficult, sometimes joyful, sometime heart-wrenching steps towards that day.

Our team, men and women who work behind the scenes, harder than any people I know work, with more soul, love, and sweat then I once thought possible.

Our Board of Directors, who ask us hard questions, support us unconditionally, and hold us to the highest integrity.

Our friends across the world, who show us that the *really*

important things—hope, love, learning—are universal and worth fighting for.

Our partners in this work, all the people who think, feel, and do good things for children.

My family, who love me no matter what, and accept that all children are my children, even when it means a little less love for them.

My brother Rishad, for living the Teach For India journey and being my greatest support through endless hours of editing numerous drafts of this book.

My Akanksha student, Teach For India Fellow, and incredible Teach For India alumnus Seema, for showing me that if you stay on the path long enough, it all makes sense. For sitting next to me through late nights of writing as she quietly did the work of a new Principal building a world-class school.

And finally, to the vision that in our lifetime, all children will attain an excellent education. This is just the beginning. There is a long path ahead.

Shaheen Mistri

Education is a powerful thing. So few of us have so much of it, and so many of us have so little of it.

My own belief in education stems from my own experiences. My dad was born in an Ahmedabad slum—there were limited opportunities available to him or his four younger siblings. Hard work and good fortune joined hands to equip him with the skills he needed. Despite attending a low-income Hindi medium school, he toiled under street lamps to make it through his classes. He found a teacher who encouraged him to apply to colleges outside India, and graduated with a Ph.D. from Purdue University.

My mom grew up in a society where girls were considered burdens; the minute they hit maturity, their marriages were fixed. Her own mother was married at 12 to a widower much older than her. My mom did not know what she would do with a college degree, only that it provided an escape from marriage. By attending college, she managed to push her marriage to the age of 20.

I did nothing special to get the opportunities that I got growing up, yet I was showered with umpteen privileges. In school, I always found teachers that believed in me. At home, I never had to worry about where my next meal would come from, or where I would find a place to sleep. Compared to other kids, I have just been lucky.

When I was in college, my uncle adopted a baby girl who had been abandoned in a plastic bag and dumped into a nearby bush in rural Rajasthan. With the child's good fate, she was eventually taken to a hospital and was christened as 'Khushi' by our family. Today, Khushi is a healthy primary school student. It took me days to get the visual of her struggling inside of that bag out of my mind. I started thinking about what would have happened if she had not got picked up that day? Or worse, what if she was picked up by a wrong pair of hands? How different would her life be today from what it is now?

I started wondering whether it was just a chance of luck that determined what sort of households we were born into. At this very crucial juncture, a Teach For India staff opportunity came into my life. As a college graduate, it was an incredible opportunity to change the way I perceived the world around me.

Teach For India strongly believes in the power of its alumni, that they will continuously impact education. Like a jigsaw puzzle, each Alumnus will pick their piece to work on. We will solve the crisis when all of these pieces come together. This book is a small yet sincere step towards playing a part in that puzzle.

Kovid Gupta

50 YEARS FROM NOW

I awoke from a dreadful dream,
Let out a loud and fearful scream.
I saw *every* child in school,
Following all the school-y rules.
They listened and listened and remembered it all,
B-a-t, bat and b-a-l-l, ball.
Their imagination and thinking was dead,
This is where their education had led.

My eyes now open,
I jump from my bed.
I thank the Lord,
And clear my head.
I want to know if my dream was the truth,
So I set out to go and meet India's youth.
I walk the path, and then I see,
Children of the world,
Happy and free.
Boys and girls,
Hands held tight.

Each one trying to find their light.
With smiles on their faces,
And a spark in their eye.
With hearts that feel,
And hands that try.
Doors are open for each child,
To bloom like flowers in the wild.
A teacher here, a parent there,
Shower kids with love and care.
Light a fire deep within,
All kids fall,
And all kids win.
Thinkers and tinkerers,
Kids question and learn.
They express themselves freely,
Know life's meaning and turn.
They pack their bags,
With values and dreams.
From me to we,
They work in teams.
Classrooms are spaces of awe and wonder,
Not jails with sticks or benches to hide under.
Teachers here bring the world inside,
Students have choices, deep and wide.

The world they live in is happy and pure,
Inventions, discoveries, diseases to cure.
All are respected and all show great care,
The world is equal; the world is fair.

A world with no boundary, division, or wall,
A world made of colors, a world for us all.

I've seen enough, I feel no fear,
I return to my bed,
For 'One Day' is here.

—Priyanka Patil, 14, Teach For India Student

CHAPTER 1

DIDI

I reached to touch a rainbow today,
I reached up high, so high.
And yet as high as I reached up,
I could not touch the sky.
I'll reach to touch a rainbow again,
I'll reach up higher than high.
And if I reach up high enough.
I just may skim the sky.*

I remember sitting on the wide verandah of our Indonesian home, writing little poems and notes in a carefully guarded diary. I would sit and watch little ants carry large loads, determined to get to their destination. What was my destiny? I was already 12-years-old, but what had I achieved?

---

* Excerpts from Shaheen's diary at 12

It was 1983, and we lived in Jakarta, in a lovely, white colonial home on a street that was quiet except for the low whistle of the Putu Man who sold steaming rice cakes rolled in fresh coconut and filled with melted palm sugar. It was a pleasant, almost perfect life, until the day I was taken to visit an orphanage in the city.

I do not remember how the orphanage looked, but I vividly remember the children. I remember especially the little boy with a head swollen so large that he could not lift it up. 'Full of water,' the orphanage staff explained to me. I guess that was the way you'd describe cerebral oedema to a 12-year-old. I saw crying children, laughing children, quiet children, screaming children, and I remember not knowing what to do. I returned to the orphanage every weekend. Perhaps it was merely curiosity, or a sense of thankfulness for all that I had, or maybe every child's real desire to learn more about the world. When I was there, I often felt sad and joyful in the same moment. I would play with the children who were able, and I would talk to the child with the heavy head.

Growing up was a whirlwind of ten schools across five countries that spanned the French, British, American, and International school systems. In my early school years, I was shy, and spent my time doing expatriate child stuff.

There were tennis lessons and school projects; a Wizard of Oz performance where I was given the tiny part of the gatekeeper to the Emerald City; sleepovers, and handcrafted birthday cakes baked by my mother. Food was important, and mum always served perfectly raised soufflés, chicken curry, Lebanese hummus, egg-white desserts and crispy meringues, the recipes borrowed from her mother, which were my favourite. Dinner conversations were sacred, moral, and political. The family was always together then. Dad would come home from his busy Citibank days to always be there. Over the years, countless guests sat at our table—architects and artists, musicians, and the many bankers that dad worked with. I'd be happy listening, but would be too shy to contribute. Music filled our lives—dad and my brother Rishad's relentless violin practice, and the regimen and benefit of having to practice piano every day. Dad's disciplined life and his personal motto of 'practice makes perfect' would be evident on Sunday mornings; when we'd wake up, he'd have already completed five productive tasks. Mum was a speech therapist and a museum educator who, in her early twenties, helped set up The Education Audiology and Research (E.A.R.) school, Mumbai's first school for the hearing-impaired. Many children would be brought into our home for therapy, and we'd watch her patiently and creatively reach out, time after time, to each child.

The bank granted its international staff two vacations a year, which gave the family, from the three continents on which we were posted, the opportunity to travel the world. As children we explored sandy coves on Greek islands and found quartz caves we truly believed were lined with diamonds, made trips to Singapore to see the dentist and the orthopedic pediatrician who sorted out my s-shaped spine, had snowy December sleighrides in the Austrian countryside, toured museums with my mother who told us lush stories of the artists lives and times, and went to incredible concerts with dad. We would wait anxiously for him to return from his many trips laden with baseball t-shirts, action figures, and Le Sportsac bags. In those days, we'd change into pyjamas in first class on the airplane, and the seats would go back as flat as a bed.

Animals were always my greatest love. I'd visit the Jakarta zoo at orangutan feeding time. There was an orphanage where baby orangutans in nappies would clutch me in tight hugs while the juveniles would try to grab our camera and occasionally even spit on us and laugh. Years later, for my favourite teacher Mr Kachuba, I completed a project and spent months at the Bronx Zoo, where I'd sit patiently in the recreated rainforest watching golden baby langurs until they grew to turn silver. Mr Kachuba had raised Siberian tigers and played in a rock band; I remember thinking even then that teachers command the greatest respect when they have the most captivating lives.

At home we had a continuous stream of pets—hamsters I'd smuggle to school, a parrot, both golden and black cocker-spaniels, a grey cat called Smokey, her brother Blackie, and a wild slow Loris that we rescued from an illegal Indonesian market and for whom we built a cage around our garden tree. It would drive me crazy when people would hurt animals. I remember overhearing the chef at the Hilton saying he was going to cook the live bunnies that were on display for Easter in the hotel lobby.

I came back to our room that day with eight little rabbits, which my parents, amazingly, let me keep. On a family vacation, my childhood friend Bryan captured a beautiful butterfly. My grandmother and I stayed awake until after Bryan was fast asleep, and then tiptoed into the room to set the butterfly free, knowing well how angry he would be in the morning. In our garden, my brother and I set up a clubhouse, decorated it with a 'No Adults' sign, and nursed stray cats, dogs, and the odd bat or mouse back to health. Animals were soft, gentle, and unconditional in their love and respect. They would shape a large part of what I now believe to be important.

I knew that Rishad was the confident, talented one; he'd try less and do better. He was Macbeth in the school play, performed on the violin at Carnegie Hall, could pick up any song by ear; I, on the other hand, would study hard and feel self-conscious. From Mumbai, my grandmother would record scary stories and mail black and yellow cassettes to Rishad and I. On her instruction, we'd first grab pillows, hold them tight, and then listen to her deliciously frightening 'scary stories'. When she would come to visit us, she would tell us stories, and sing us her favourite old songs. She loved watching us giggle as she covered her mouth with her hand, opened her eyes wide, and sang, 'I walked past your window and saw you undress, you took off your nightie and stood in your vest!' I think my belief in the power of songs and stories came from her.

I began to understand that life wasn't perfect during my summer vacations. My summers were spent between the orphanage in Jakarta and trips back to Mumbai where I volunteered at The Happy Home and School for the Blind.

I was struck by the potential apparent in little Mariappa — whose albino skin turned so quickly pink in the sun — with his wide smile and crinkled joy in his blind eyes. I saw how Vivek came to life when a teacher played music, and spent hours trying unsuccessfully to mold wet clay on an electric pottery wheel. I remember thinking of the beauty you can create when you look beyond what you can see. The school buzzed with confident children running up and down staircases, or playing cricket on the terrace with a ball that jingled. During the Ganpati festival, the boys loved making the elaborately decorated elephant idol each year and danced around it through the night.

At fourteen, I volunteered at the school for the hearing impaired that my mum helped found years ago in Bombay, and I was struck by the importance of communication. Two years later, I spent a difficult summer at a school for autistic teenagers in New York. I remember the boys being taller and stronger than me, and when they were out of control, I remember feeling so small, and just helpless.

It was through these summer experiences that I began to see inequity. I'd go from a family lunch to the dining hall at the blind school; I'd watch through the window of my air-conditioned car, as children would beg in the streets. I'd see piles of wasted food at a friend's party and when I left, I would notice a woman, sitting on the side of the road, portioning out all-too meagre amounts of dal and rice for her family. I started to see the slums of Mumbai as the fabric of the city; suddenly they appeared to be everywhere. I started seeing the children, some less than half my age, selling magazines and sweet-smelling mogra bracelets on the streets late into the night. I began to notice the disparity that existed in different people's lives. These summers were short however, and soon I'd be back in the whirlwind of my private school reality.

As a teenager I was still very shy, but was also starting to be truly disturbed at the unequal distribution of opportunity. It didn't seem fair that I was born with so much when others did not have enough. I began to feel this more and more, and in this realization I began to find my voice. In listening, learning, and understanding about the nature of this inequity, I began to speak more.

By the time I turned 16, I was at Greenwich Academy, a world-class school for some of the most privileged girls in the United States. Our graduating class had 60 girls, many of whom had probably known which ivy-league college they wanted to attend from the time they could first speak. I was the only Indian in my class. Conversations around birthdays centred not on *whether* they'd get a car for their 16th birthday, but on *which* car they'd get. We did the usual teenager stuff—talked about the boys we liked, kept secret diaries, agonized over the white gowns we'd buy for our school graduation ceremony. Somewhere, my summer confidence seeped over into my school year. When someone in our school threw a rock at a classmate's car, shattering her windscreen, I surprised myself by standing up at the school assembly, sharing thoughts on what it meant to have the integrity not to defend a friend who was wrong.

After Greenwich Academy, I attended Tufts University in 1988 and planned to major in Early Childhood Development. Like my friends, I thought I was on a path to a predictable life. I'd get a secure degree, a high-paying job, and have a strong marriage. I'd send my kids to a good college so that they could in turn get a high-paying job, thus perpetuating the cycle. Little did I know that wasn't how it would play out.

I went back to Mumbai in the summer of 1989. The family vacation began with the usual rounds of welcome lunches and dinner parties. I returned to the School for the Blind, met the wonderful kids I knew there, and caught up on local gossip with my cousins. At the end of that summer, my parents left for the US, leaving me to spend an extra week with my cousins before returning to my second year at Tufts.

It was in that week that everything changed for me. On one blistering Mumbai day my taxi stopped at a traffic signal in the business district. Three children ran up to my window, smiling and begging, and in that moment I had a flash of introspection. Nothing too unusual had happened, but as I looked at them, I suddenly knew that my life would have more meaning if I stayed in India. I saw potential in that fleeting moment — in the children at my open window and in myself. The signal turned green and the taxi started up again. We left the three children on the road there, just standing.

In the days that followed, I kept thinking about those kids and that moment. India was answering the search for purpose that I had felt ever since I was a child. I was being challenged to find my identity; I wanted to be part of making things better for children. I knew then that this could be my country, and that whatever I did here could make more of a difference than in the manicured reality of my university life in the States.

At 18, I did not think of the quality education I'd forego by leaving Tufts, nor the fact that I didn't speak a word of

Hindi. Although born in India, I had grown up abroad in an exclusively English-speaking Zoroastrian family. I didn't even think about the family and friends I'd leave behind by making this drastic change; instead, I just knew that India was the place where I would make my life.

Nervously, a week before I was to return to Boston, I telephoned my parents to try and explain the jumbled feelings that culminated in my strong desire to move back to Mumbai. They listened carefully, but advised me to complete my undergraduate degree at Tufts and then to consider returning to India. They cautioned that living in Mumbai would be vastly different from my current vacation. They talked to me of the value of a Tufts University education. They pointed out that I did not speak an Indian language. My parents had both grown up in Bombay and had seen the progression and harsh realities of the city's slums, and gave me their insight with regards to the enormity of the problem. But when I persisted, they agreed — on two conditions: that I would get admission into a good undergraduate college in the city, and later I would travel abroad for my graduate degree. I was thrilled to get their tentative approval, although knowing my rebellious nature, I might well have stayed anyway. And now that this was actually happening, I was also more than a little daunted about what lay ahead.

The only place I could think to start was St. Xavier's, where my parents had studied. I walked into the crowded college office and asked for an appointment to see the Principal. 'Admissions shut three months earlier', I was told, and 'the Principal doesn't *give* appointments'. I must have felt I had a lot at stake, and, for a moment, I saw it all ending before it began. I stood in the corridor outside the office, choking back frustration. A student standing in the outside office witnessed the exchange between the Principal's assistant and me. He came over and whispered with a wink, 'There's a side door to the Principal's office. You may want to try that.' Here was another moment I will always be grateful for, and a lesson that the small, kind things we do can be catalysts to so significantly impact the lives of others for the better.

I went straight through the side door. Father D'Cruz sat behind a wooden desk wide enough to be a ship. He looked up quizzically and opened his mouth, but before he could say anything I blurted out what I had rehearsed; 'Father, my life is in your hands. I want to do something for the children of India. I don't know how, only that I must.' I'm not quite sure what he must have thought of the overtly fervent request in my mixed-up accent, but it made him curious enough to ask me a few questions. At the end of our short conversation, despite the fact that admissions was closed, the Father thankfully granted me admission to St. Xavier's College.

The academic system at Xavier's was different than the system at Tufts. Xavier's did not offer a major in Education so I chose Sociology, thinking I'd learn a little more about what India really was. Here a far more bookish form of learning replaced the academic rigor and intellectual stimulation I had received in Massachusetts. One of my Xavier professors would repeat each line from the textbook three times, saying 'I repeat' after each line, while we'd copy down what he said. I tried to be Indian in many ways, wearing cotton sarees and brightly coloured round bindis, until people began to ask if

I was a professor. I quickly realized that I'd be able to learn more in the city beyond the classroom.

Now that I lived in India, I wanted to understand it in a different and deeper way than I had during my summer holidays. I walked around the city, just watching and listening. I spent many hours on Chowpatty beach absorbing the life in Mumbai. I decided to go to the *Times of India* to apply for an internship. When they told me that they didn't hire interns, I asked a reporter, Rajiv, to allow me to follow him around. Luckily, he agreed. Through him I got access to police stations, jails, the courthouse, and juvenile remand homes. One day, when I looked particularly overwhelmed, he sat down with me in a small South Indian restaurant. 'What's the population of India?' he asked, as he handed me a pencil and small piece of paper. I wrote down '840 million.' He then took back the pencil and wrote down the number '1' above the 840 as a fraction. 1/840 million. 'That's your role,' he said. 'Never forget that. Do that well. Anything you do above that is great.'

~

I walked into a sprawling, low-income community within a short walking distance from my grandmother's apartment. The community was a maze of tiny alleyways, buzzing with life. There were tiny carts, where women sold raw fish in the hot sunlight just a few feet away from a massive festering garbage dump. Every time we walked through one part of the community, we had to keep our mouths closed to keep the flies out. Half-naked children would run around barefoot, playing with an old tire, a few pebbles, or a torn kite. An estimated 10,000 people lived here with no running water, no system of waste disposal, and shared six dark cubicle toilets that lined an adjoining alley.

That first day, overwhelmed by the stench, disoriented by the noise and dust, I saw Pinky. She must have been around six or seven, and stood, spine straight, wearing white shorts that were three sizes too big for her, and a dark brown t-shirt three sizes too small. Her oily hair shined, tied back tightly, and kajal lined her huge, almond-shaped eyes that struck me as bottomless, which for me became so symbolic of the limitless potential in every child.

I walked around that afternoon speaking with children, wondering how life would be different if each one of them only had access to the opportunities that would fill their greatest potential. Walking down the narrow passageways, I must have looked a little dazed, when a soft-spoken girl dressed in a beautiful sari welcomed me into her home. Sandhya was also eighteen and didn't speak a word of English, but she smiled and laughed a lot, and I felt an immediate connection with her. She laughed at my attempt to learn a few words of Hindi, at my request to learn to roll a round chapatti, and at my curiosity about everything in her life. She lived with her elderly mother, who welcomed me in with earnest kindness, promptly fed me, and chatted non-stop with me as though we had been friends for years; all despite the fact that I couldn't understand a word of what she was saying. Sandhya's life was just so different from mine.

I would leave college each day after that, often skipping my last lecture, to go to Sandhya's little, ten-by-ten foot home which also housed her mother and her mentally challenged brother. Sandhya's home was smaller than the bathroom at my grandmother's, but when a few children poked their heads inside the doorway to say hi to us, she welcomed them in. These children eventually formed the first class I would teach. Each day a few more kids would crowd into the little home and ask to learn a few words in English, or ask to learn a little math, or a song. In a few days, the kids would start to request other things—help filling out a school admission form, or advice on how to navigate a government hospital. Even though I knew very little of India, I felt useful and confident.

This became my routine. I'd leave college as soon as I could and rush to my new world in the community. Here I saw truth and hope. There was little Sonu's newborn brother, introduced to me with so much pride. A week later he died of suspected diarrhoea or dysentery. The thought of how a little help would have prevented this infant's death kept ringing in my mind. There was 7-year-old Nagesh, who had a growth on the side of his neck the size of an orange, making him tilt his head at an almost right angle. Superstition made his mother believe that this was a curse and that the *Devi* resided in him. I remember days of frustration trying to explain to her that her son needed a doctor badly, and the rush of relief when she finally agreed to take him to one. There was Gitanjali and Bharki, both age six, and both best friends until the day a fight between their mothers went out of control and Gitanjali's mother poured hot kerosene on Bharki's mother. It was twelve o'clock in the afternoon in the crowded community and nobody intervened. Bharki's mother was burned to death, and Gitanjali's was taken to jail. What would it take to give Sonu, Nagesh, Bharki, and Gitanjali the belief that this world made sense? There were also the little children who started to come to our informal class regularly—mischievous Shakeel, quiet Sameena, bright-eyed Parveen. 'Didi, Didi!' they would shout excitedly. And for a few hours, we'd forget the dark side of the community, immersing ourselves in laughter and learning.

~

Six months later, I asked myself what I was doing. What would happen to my kids if I went back to Tufts University? Who was I doing this for? Was it making a difference or was I just feeling better about myself and making a few people dependent on me in the process? I still had the opportunity to go back to Tufts after I had deferred a year, and I knew it was time to decide whether this had just been an interesting project, or whether it was something more. I took a week to think, flew to Riyadh where my parents now lived, and asked myself these questions. Sitting in the large, quiet walled-in house, I thought about what I had seen, heard, and felt. I thought about what it felt like to be called 'Shaheen Didi'. A week later, I flew back to India, knowing that I'd never go back to Tufts. It was 1991, and this was starting to feel like a lifelong commitment.

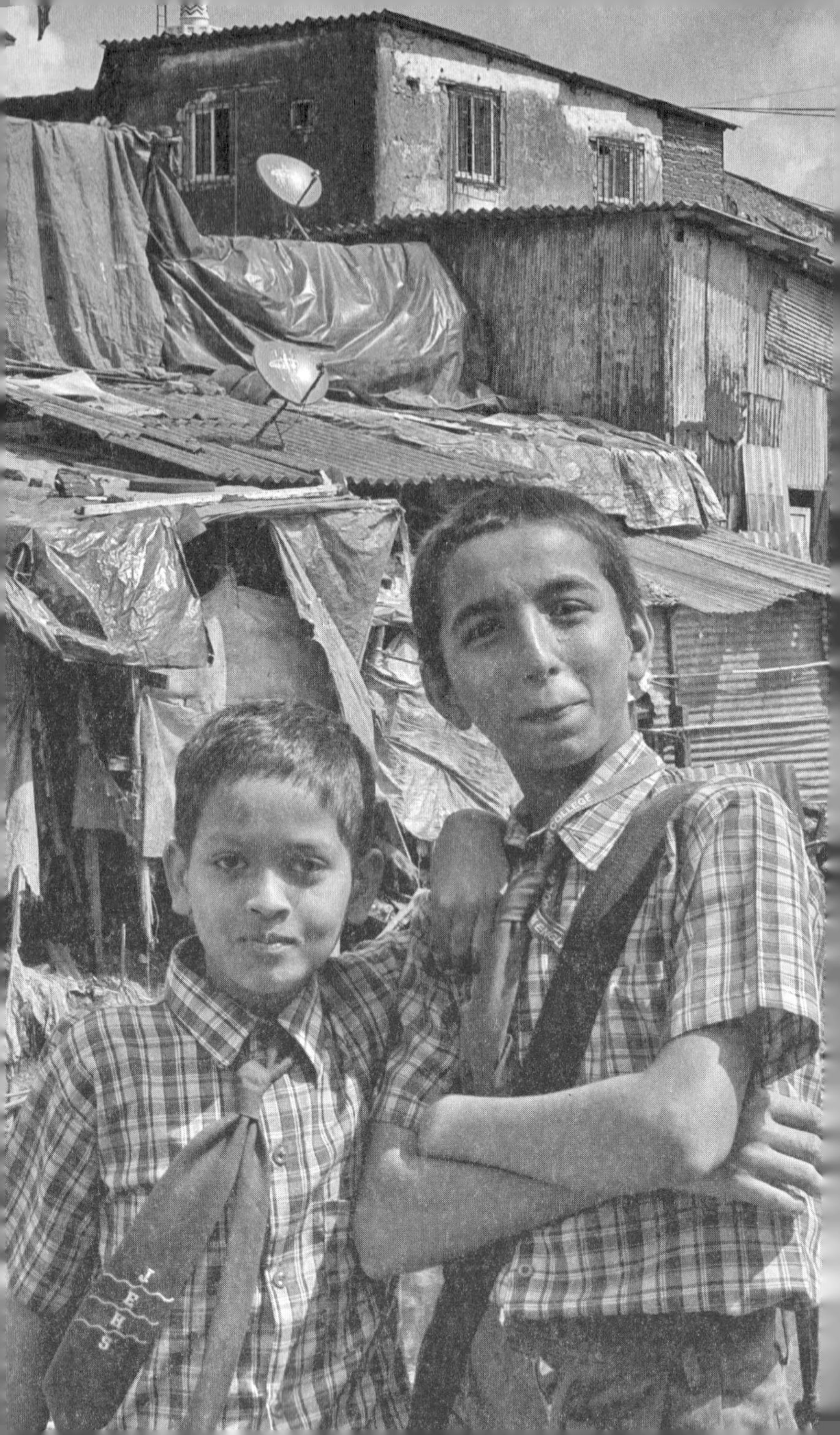
COLLEGE
J
E
H
S

CHAPTER 2

WE WILL RISE

You may look down upon us because we are from the slums,
But we'll rise like educated people,
And show the world that we can do something in life.
You may criticize us,
You may try to stop us from achieving our goals,
And force us to give up,
But we will face you and rise.

You may treat us badly,
Making fun of us, teasing us,
Discriminating in groups,
But we will rise.
You may separate us,
You may hate us or ignore us,
But with love we will rise.
We will rise, we will rise, we will rise.

In spite of the discouraging neighbourhood,
And conservative background,
We will rise like the day that comes after every night.

You may brainwash us by taunting us,
But instead we will learn how to fly in the sky.
In the sky flying high,
Like a bird,
In freedom of the light.
We will rise. We will rise. We will rise.*

—Akanksha Students: Sagar, Shyam, Chandrakala, Shehnaz, Vijay, Ajay S, Shakila, Stella, Jyoti, Dinesh, Nazir

---

* From a class activity where the children were asked to write a poem based on Maya Angelou's poem 'We Will Rise'

'Shaheen Didi started teaching classes through a project called Akanksha. Sometimes, she did not have classrooms so she used to teach in gardens, or even on the roads. I never attended her classes; I just used to go and drop off my brother. One day, Didi came inside our home and asked my parents for permission to take me with her.

'It must have been hard for Didi. She looked like a foreigner, so different from the rest of us. Everyone doubted her in the beginning. They did not trust her; they assumed she was gathering the children for her own benefit. They thought that she would click photographs and showcase them in newspapers and on television. It was so hard for her to convince people to let go of their children. Over time, all of the parents saw that her intentions were real.

'Until Didi came into my life, I used to shiver at the thought of a teacher. A teacher to me meant one who intimidates and beats you. I never thought of a teacher as someone who could love and motivate you.'

—Naheeda Ansari, Akanksha Alumnus and
Akanksha Teacher

Akanksha was born of the simple idea that India had people who could teach, spaces that could be utilized as classrooms, and the funds with which to educate *all* her children. That India's most valuable natural resources were the agile minds and open hearts of her children, who desperately needed an education, and the thousands of bright young college students who could be mobilized to teach them. Shaheen believed that, despite Mumbai's population of 16 million people, the city must have under-utilized spaces that could be put to use as classrooms. *Everything exists*, she thought, *I just need to find a way to bring it all together.*

With her college friend Jeshry, Shaheen asked 300 people who lived in the community what their biggest challenges and greatest hopes were. Again and again they heard the same three things—housing, water, and education. 'We want our children to be in a good school, Didi,' they said.

Shaheen realized that if she wanted her small group of students to take school seriously, they needed an environment free of the community's distractions. School needed to stay in session, even if a little girl was required to collect water for her family or if a young boy fell ill. They'd need to move out of Sandhya's ten-foot home.

Here started the search for the first Akanksha Centre space. Shaheen approached school Principals all over the city, requesting they give her one classroom in their school buildings for three hours every evening. She promised to clean the classrooms each day and carry all her teaching materials home each evening. Some administrators claimed that her idea to educate underprivileged children was way too 'revolutionary,' while others complained that they would spread diseases to the other students. A nun at a reputable convent school even complained how she simply couldn't allow the children into her school, as the glass bangles worn by the daughters of fishermen would scratch the desks of her classrooms.

Shaheen visited twenty schools and experienced repeated disappointments. Each incident reinforced what Shaheen was coming to know—that the toughest part of educating India's children would not be teaching, it would be changing the mindsets of the people who believed that these children could not succeed. Almost ready to give up, Shaheen visited the Holy Name High School in Colaba. She entered into the meeting with the school's Principal, Father Ivo D'Souza, remembering what had worked so well with Father D'Cruz when she had attempted to get admission into Xavier's:

'Father, my life is in your hands...'

She asked for the bare minimum: one classroom, no storage area, and no use of the bathroom. Her only request from him was the physical space where she could teach her kids. She did not require desks or chairs. And she would bring her own mop and broom to clean the class. Father Ivo agreed and asked her when she would like to start. Afraid that he may change his mind, Shaheen committed to starting the very next day.

Relieved she had a classroom, Shaheen wasn't sure how, or even if, her children would come to class; the school was a long walk from Sandhya's community, and there was no school bus. Shaheen had no teachers, no curriculum, and no supplies. All she had was 24 hours to figure out how to get the children to school.

That evening, Shaheen sourced a school bus and raised the funds from friends and family to rent it. This bus remained Akanksha's only expense for the next four years. She rallied her friends at Xavier's, most of whom were not even marginally interested in being educators, and pleaded with them to teach for a few days until she was able to mobilize volunteers. 'If you don't love children,' she said with a smile, 'pretend.' She thought back to what she found most interesting as a student, and quickly developed a rough plan of what they'd teach. *I have to keep it fun*, she thought, *to keep it interactive. Ask questions. Colour. Work in teams. Get the children to sing, dance, and learn through games. Make class a place the children can feel safe; a space they can leave the difficulties of their lives behind and just be children.* Some of those initial ideas would shape Akanksha's educational philosophy for years to come.

Each day would start hours before school. Shaheen would walk through the maze of narrow gullies in the community, reminding children to attend class, and helping them to get ready. Excitedly, the children would dab their faces with powder, smile their biggest smiles, and follow Shaheen down a winding line through the alleyways to the edge of the community where the newly rented bus would be waiting to pick them up. Fifteen students, aged three to fourteen, jumped on the bus, and many more would crowd around asking if they could come. Some of the children would run after the bus, clinging to the bumpers and door handles as it pulled out and started down the road. Shaheen looked back at them jumping and waving. There were an infinite number of children who were hungry for an education, for someone to lead them away from the community, even if for a little while.

~

The fifteen children who had been attending class were selected to come to the Holy Name School. For them, learning would start immediately, right there on the bus. The children sang songs, looked out of the window, and learnt from the things they saw. The children walked in a line from the bus, past the Cathedral of the Holy Name and up the flight of steps that would take them to their new school of shiny, heavy wooden desks and bathrooms that had running water. This just thrilled the children.

Back at Xavier's College, Shaheen spent her time recruiting volunteers. She would walk around the canteen asking students, 'What angers you most about India?' 'So much', they'd often reply. She couldn't understand. 'If so much bothers you, why aren't you doing anything about it?' They all responded: 'The problems are just too big. What difference can *I* make?'

Over curry rice and cups of coffee, she'd explain again and again how one person *could* make the difference. Shaheen requested her professors for five minutes of time during each college lecture, and walked into rooms full of college students with hand-painted posters that said, 'Together, we can make a difference. Come, Teach!' Slowly, people started listening.

The early days of Akanksha were filled with a million things that certainly did *not* seem like they were making a difference. On most days, the children would break out of the line and race to the bathrooms, jump into the large white basins, turn the all the taps on full, and get drenched in the deliciously clean water, squealing with laughter. School was less about learning and more about who could throw clay on the ceiling and hilariously watch when it would fall on their Didi's head. The children didn't come to study; they came to shout, run around, and be free. There would always be one or two volunteers at the end of the day in tears, and invariably someone would say to Shaheen, 'you said we would make a difference. What difference can we possibly be making?' This slowly turned into a vicious cycle difficult to break: demotivated volunteers led to children not learning; unruly children led to demotivated volunteers.

'I learnt that challenges don't actually motivate most people; they needed success in order to feel that their efforts were worthwhile.' Shaheen surmised that people were drawn to the mission from their own perspective, and for their own reasons; everyone didn't necessarily have the desire to change children's lives, or find where they could have maximum impact to effect positive change. Some volunteers simply wanted extra college credit, or a compelling line on their resume. But if the volunteers were showing up at school and helping with the children, Shaheen was grateful.

A regular group of volunteers now began to come together as a team. They would visit each other's homes on Sundays, borrowing each other's kurtas and plan lessons, making lists of creative activities, and drawing up class timetables. They sat together to plan for what Akanksha would come to be. Shaheen would recall,

'We needed a name, so sitting around one afternoon in college, we each put our ideas on a slip of paper and into a hat. When we opened them, everyone loved the name Rachna had chosen, 'Akanksha', meaning aspiration, or hope. Another volunteer, Neha, offered to ask her sister to design the logo and thus the first version of the Akanksha sun was born. Akanksha. Hope. The Sun. Potential. Things were starting to make sense together.'

~

At the same time, the volunteers were spending more time in the community, learning more about the needs of the children who lived there. Many of these children's families had migrated from their villages—both here in Maharashtra and in other states throughout India. They had left rural villages and towns, often generations earlier, in search of employment in Mumbai. The children's parents worked as rag pickers, fisher-folk, construction site workers, or vendors in the tiny shops that dotted the community. The slum was rife with drinking and gambling rooms where many of the men spent their time, which often resulted in extreme financial and emotional pressure on the mothers, who also worked as maids in upper income households, sometimes right across the road but in a vastly different city. These circumstances often resulted in rampant domestic violence that victimized both the mothers and their children.

One day Shaheen saw a mother angrily beating a bathing child as she rounded up her students before school. When she stopped to talk to the mother, she realized that the little child was crying because soap was in her eyes. The child had done nothing wrong. Like so many parents, this mother's frustration with the hardship of her own life resulted in her anger at her weeping child. Shaheen remembers the depth of hardship and pain cut into the deep lines on her mother's face. This was not a vicious woman; instead, this mother was a victim of an inequity that was so much larger than her.

There were harsh realities to contend with in the community. A girl was heard screaming. Rushing through the dim snaking passageways toward the sound, Shaheen saw 13-year-old Sunita's clothes and hair were on fire. Sunita was mentally challenged and had been left alone at home. Her nylon dress had caught fire while she was cooking. As Shaheen rushed to get a taxi to take her to hospital, Sunita alternated between laughing maniacally and sobbing hysterically; she had completely broken down and lost control of herself. For the next fifteen days, Shaheen spent most of her time in the large municipal hospital ward with Sunita, who had sustained burns on 80 percent of her body. Sunita's mother earned daily wages, which meant the days she didn't work, her family would have to go without food. Devastated, she came to the hospital whenever possible. Numb, sitting next to Shaheen, she said that she thought it would be better if her daughter died. 'She didn't have a life even before this,' she said. 'What life can she possibly have now?' Shaheen wondered what could have happened to lead a mother into such a desperate situation so that she really believed her own child to be better off dead than alive. Would it have made a difference if Sunita had access to the bare bones of a good education, the kind that taught her how to stay safe and look after herself? Would her mother have left her alone to cook if she had been educated herself on the special needs of her child? Would this tragedy have happened if a teacher, who simply believed in Sunita's potential, had been present in her life?

Being exposed to these experiences in the community fuelled a palpable urgency in the young volunteers at the Akanksha centre. They had once lived across the economic divide from where they had looked at the community but had not seen it. The emotional roar, which came from these very real family tragedies, now deafened them. Their children's family's needs were now apparent, and urgent. There was so much to do and the lives of their children were so frighteningly fragile and depended upon their success.

> 'When I met my group of 12-year-olds for the first time, I assumed they knew some things that every Indian, affluent or penniless, should know. I felt like someone punched me in my stomach when they asked me, "Didi, who is Gandhi?" I was shocked. How was it acceptable that a 12-year-old child did not know the Father of our Nation? I once thought every Indian was brought up with some basic knowledge, but in reality, not all of us have the opportunity to learn even the most basic things.'
>
> —Anjali Sabnani, former Akanksha Teacher and Director, Education, Akanksha

Volunteers started with the basics. They cut little black-rimmed nails, combed hair into pretty plaits, banned bad language, and taught the children to sit 'beautifully'. Classroom management was a huge challenge, and it would take just seconds for a class that was seemingly on task to break into chaos. When the second Akanksha Centre started, this time at Xavier's College, six teachers resigned in a single year. Most teachers didn't know what to do when children fought, showed disrespect to them, or fell asleep in class. Most volunteers had come from a different world, one that they had left for just a few hours to teach here, and when they didn't feel they were getting results and their patience was sufficiently tested, they'd drop out. It was hard to make the switch from a carefree college student who attended structured, disciplined lectures to a teacher, a person responsible for children's lives.

Rajshree Doshi, a volunteer at the Akanksha centre, was different. Somewhere close to the time when the sixth teacher left, she came to Shaheen and asked if she could be the teacher. 'Six teachers have come and gone,' Shaheen said, 'how are you sure you can do this?' Rajshree looked at Shaheen with her disarming smile. 'It doesn't seem like you have a line of teachers waiting to teach this class. Are you *really* in a position to say no?' Rajshree's belief struck Shaheen. 'I *know* that these children will listen to me,' she said. 'Give me a chance.' Within three months, Rajshree had Naheeda, Naval, Babu, Sangeeta, among many others, all completely invested in their learning. She believed in them, adored them, and made them believe that they could change their lives. She would help them get through any challenge, in or out of class.

'If you walked along P. D'Mello Road, you would have seen the shanties dotting the road where our children lived. During the monsoon, the municipality would destroy our children's homes, leaving them on wet footpaths without

a roof over their heads. Our children would miss class—some were caring for their baby siblings, others were fainting from hunger. Many were trying to rebuild their homes using scraps of tin and plastic.

'All we wanted was to get them under a roof. Education was not important at that point, basic human survival was. Fires were not burning in their homes and the kids were starving. We took cars and taxis and rounded up our children and their toddler siblings to keep them dry under the roof of the Holy Name School. Then we went to Mumbai's 5-star hotels; they threw away their leftover lunch food at 3 pm. Hotels like the Taj and the Oberoi blessed us. They gave us fruit and bread that we supplied to the children. Sometimes we gave them boiled potatoes. We did not pity the children; we just wanted to keep them going. They were our responsibility.'

—Rajshree Doshi, former Akanksha Teacher, School Coach at Akanksha and Teach For India Coach

As volunteers understood their children's lives, they learnt about inequity. Having a bathroom at home was now a luxury; running water was magical while having space to be alone felt indulgent. Instead, the children woke up early to complete household chores, queued up in long lines to fill heavy buckets of water, faced suffocating heat and pollution, and were always surrounded by the city's endless street noise. The monsoons were especially difficult, with incidents of illnesses rising. Over the years, several children contracted diseases that spread through the existence of stagnant water and generally unhygienic conditions. Over the years, a few children would die of suspected leptospirosis and other diseases.

~

Shaheen and the other volunteers began to learn more about teaching. They learnt to always love them as children first, and to teach them as students next. She carried a few packets of Parle-G biscuits to school each day for the kids who came hungry. Meanwhile, volunteers combed hair, pinned on handkerchiefs, and found donated t-shirts so the children would have a uniform, just like all the other school children in the city. In the beginning, to save money, volunteers would hand paint the Akanksha sun logo on more than 500 bright yellow t-shirts. Hair brushed, nails cut, and t-shirts proudly painted, the students would be ready to learn. Volunteers would choose a theme, and all subjects would be taught through that theme. The first was with the theme *'Me'*, where the children were encouraged to discover themselves. They drew self-portraits, outlined their bodies on newspaper, and then wrote about themselves. The themes moved from *'Things that are close to me'* to *'Things that are far from me'*. From family, friends, class, community, to their city, country, and the world. The children 'experienced' a new religion each week, with a student sharing about his or her religion, teaching the class a prayer or song, bringing in traditional clothes and other artifacts. The class would visit places of religious worship and celebrate diversity. The project ended with students creating three-dimensional models of different religions and thinking critically about the differences and similarities in religion. Art, values, and academics came together in those early classes at Akanksha.

As the teaching improved, the learning did too. As new levels of discipline slowly began to manifest, classes were better managed and the attention to learning increased. Volunteers became important role models who could provide their children with a changed life vision. The more they got to know the children, the more they gave of themselves to their work at Akanksha. Their students became their role models too. At one Christmas party held at the Parsi Gymkhana, all the children were given an ice-cream stick but one of the little boys refused to eat it. When asked why, he said he wanted to take it home to share it with his sister. He was 5-years-old.

> 'As part of an assignment in a teacher's meeting, we were asked to go spend a couple of hours talking to a child on the streets. I spent my time with Salman. He was thirteen and he told me about his life selling books at crowded traffic signals, about narrowly escaping wire-tied canes used by the police, and about how sometimes the municipality would come and throw their books into the water. I was floored by his attitude to life. When I asked how he felt seeing people whizzing by in big cars, his response was, "They belong where they are, I where I am. We all have our own places. We should be happy with where we are. In fact, I feel I am happier and luckier than them. They have such huge cars to take them to places and yet they are always in a hurry. So much that they keep honking even when the traffic signal is red." When asked what makes him sad, he replied, "Why do you want

me to think about what is not happy? I am happy just the way I am".'

—Caroline Nagar, former Akanksha Teacher and School Coach, Akanksha

Salman wanted badly to study and so Caroline invited him to class. In four years, he went from learning two times tables and basic words in English to passing his 10th standard exams. He went on to score 81 percent in his 12th standard board exams, and got admission into K.C. College of Arts, a top Mumbai College. He believed his life could change, and it did. Salman would become a real support to Caroline, and through difficult times would remind her to stay focused on all that she had in her life, and not on what she did not.

Now, almost twenty, Shaheen found a small room just big enough for one desk under the staircase of the boys' hostel at St. Xavier's college, which became the Akanksha office. She quickly learnt she had to use time effectively; the children had years of learning to catch up on, while she had only two and a half hours a day with them. She asked volunteers to come in early, and lay out trays with all their materials so that each of the 150 minutes of class time could be utilized effectively. Every day ended with a discussion on how the day had been, and what they could do differently to make a better tomorrow.

~

Four years after Akanksha began, Shaheen wanted to move from a volunteer-run organization to a more formally structured one. There seemed enough momentum to make this change happen, without taking away from the drive and inspiration that the founding volunteers had fostered. They had already begun to see significant changes in their students. The first centres had shown that children from the lowest strata of society could learn at high levels, and this fuelled the team to want to do more.

To ensure Akanksha could have more impact in the future, it needed to be formalized, and Shaheen knew that strengthening her own formal knowledge base would serve that end. She left for Manchester University to do a Masters' Degree in Educational Project Planning and Development, hoping to return to India with answers to some of the many questions that had arisen at Akanksha on curriculum, teaching methodology, and systems of fund-raising. Akanksha's annual budget consisted of the Rs 20,000 that it cost to rent the bus, and Shaheen needed very different fund raising strategies to replace her current conversations with friends and family. Completing her graduate degree was also a promise she had made to her parents. The course was less than twelve months in duration, and her close friend Arati would be there to manage Akanksha while she was gone. Arati promised to write almost daily letters to her with detailed Akanksha updates, reassuring Shaheen that she would do whatever it took to get the children to school. It made sense to go.

'There are more than 32 kids in school every day. Most of them come out on their own, but some still need to be pulled out every day from the community.'

— Arati Menon Gupta, former Akanksha Teacher

During those twelve months at Manchester, Shaheen volunteered at a low-income school. Their teacher asked the 7th standard students to read Shakespeare but instead they chose to throw plastic coke bottles at each other and refused to sit next to people of different religions. They were reading years below grade level. Their teacher sat with his legs propped up on his desk, and a blank look that said that he had given up. Shaheen thought about what it must have taken for this teacher, and these children, to get to this unfathomable place. This problem was obviously global.

Shaheen's international upbringing, her education at Manchester, and the many fascinating educators she met there provided her a platform to strategically map out where the future of Akanksha would lead. She wrote her M.Ed. thesis on 'the Role of India's College Students in India's Educational Development'. In this thesis was the seed that would lead to the creation of Teach For India two decades later.

~

To impact less privileged children by enabling them to maximize their potential and change their lives. With the mission in place, Shaheen set out to register The Akanksha Foundation as a formal entity, hire her first teachers, find the spaces to start new Akanksha Centres and raise the funds to run them.

Setting up a non-profit in India was a tiresome affair. Cases of fraud and unethical treatment of the less privileged had led the government, with just cause, to be wary of start-up NGOs. In the early 90s the law stated that a non-profit had to be established for three years, with a proven track record in order to get tax exemptions for its donors. This made it challenging to raise funds. The red tape in the bureaucratic system further slowed down the processing of applications. The number of social entrepreneurs was few, and there was no precedent of young college graduates founding non-profits.

Shaheen would make countless trips to the Mumbai charity commissioner's office where files were stacked from floor to ceiling. Each time she thought her application was complete, they would ask for yet another document. Overwhelmed, she asked Colonel Gupta, a friend's father, to help. He would patiently explain the system to her, and would accompany her to the government offices until she finally was able to register Akanksha as a Charitable Trust. Akanksha's first Trustees were all students from St. Xavier's College.

Talking to government officials and donors was difficult, as Shaheen was still the shy girl from her childhood. A decade earlier, she would ask her brother Rishad for help on the simplest tasks; now she needed to ask for thousands of rupees. Fund-raising did not come naturally to her; nonetheless it was a skill she would develop. Akanksha needed to hire full-time teachers and rent buses to bring children from the communities to the centres. Shaheen had to learn to tell her story, and share the dream of Akanksha in a way that would make sense to a wide group of people. She started with the Citibank family; friends of her parents who had seen first-hand the passion with which she lived Akanksha.

'It is in those moments when I lose confidence that I think of Rafiqul, who walked into one of our classrooms a few years back. For one month, he did not speak a word. Not to any of his classmates, not to any of the other teachers, not to me. He would come to class, do what the other children did, but he would not, or could not, speak.

'One month later, Rafiqul raised his hand. Hesitatingly, he pushed himself to walk to the front of the classroom, and finally spoke his first word. I remember the smile break on his face that day when the class erupted into applause. Fifteen years later, walking on Marine Drive, I heard someone shout out my name. I turned and saw Rafiqul beaming on his motorcycle. "Didi!" he called out.

'I often think of the incredible courage that little Rafiqul had to muster up that day in class, as he made that walk to the front of the class and spoke his first words. And that gives me confidence.'

Shaheen overcame the discomfort she felt when asking for money by fundamentally changing the way she thought about charitable donations. In a conversation with Rachna Mathur, Akanksha's first teacher, at the services club in Mumbai, she suddenly realized that she wasn't raising money for herself. Rachna proposed a 'Sponsor-a-Centre' scheme, which would ask a donor for two lakhs a year, and in return give them the ability to have their own Akanksha Centre. They could come and meet the children, volunteer occasionally, and take them on field trips. They could be real partners. What had seemed an insurmountable task now seemed creative, fun, and personal.

While looking for donors to fund the growing number of centres, money came in from countless individuals as well. Shaheen's neighbours, the three young Bharucha sisters once saved up their pocket money, rupee by rupee, and made a donation. People also chose to celebrate special occasions with Akanksha, hosting a birthday party with our children, sponsoring a special meal to celebrate a death anniversary. Others donated biscuits for children that came hungry, iron capsules for the mothers of our students, or free stationary and school supplies for Akanksha to use. On weekends, Citibank allowed Akanksha volunteers to use its photocopy machines to make worksheets and handouts.

Shaheen was overwhelmed by the trust and generosity she received from so many people. She realized that there were people from every sector who really wanted to do their part to help. This generosity also placed tremendous responsibility on the small team. They needed to do everything possible to keep and build the faith that people had in them, and the dreams they saw for their children. That meant that they had to function as professionals; they'd need to learn fast. Step-by-step, the team was able to learn things ranging from writing annual reports to managing finances.

After four years of running Akanksha on the good will of the volunteers, Shaheen realized the need for a paid, full-time team. Here again the learning curve was steep. How much did she need to pay them? Who and where were these people? Why would they join? Initially, she was somewhat intimidated when Rachna, her first teacher, came into their little office and interviewed *her*, instead of the other way around. She chose her early teachers carefully, less for their skill and more for their sincerity, belief, and love for children.

The Akanksha teachers decided to focus on English, Math, and Values. English would give the Akanksha students access to high quality colleges and open up opportunities for employment. Math would teach them problem-solving and critical thinking. Values would give them a strong internal compass, and also reinforce to the children that they had so much to give to others. At first the curriculum was rudimentary, but it kept getting better. Shaheen looked at conventional Indian textbooks and supplemented them with worksheets, activities, projects, and assessments. From the beginning, all forms of the Arts were integrated into the classroom. Shaheen found a tucked-away Montessori toymaker, borrowed a system to teach Math using manipulatives, and brought in movies for the children to see. The children would celebrate each other's religious festivals together, and parents would come in to class regularly. 'Show and Tell' was the exciting moment where a child would sit on an elaborately decorated seat and share anything at all that they felt they wanted to with the class.

Teaching in a second, sometimes third language was challenging and the team found creative solutions. 'Speak English' was printed on the back of brightly coloured t-shirts so that students would remember to use English in class. The classroom was covered in words, allowing students to quickly learn familiar words on sight. Teachers would funnily walk around labeled with the words 'head', 'legs', 'back' for children to learn the parts of their bodies. Students would be asked to 'find' words on their way home. Roleplays created real-life situations, and the *idea* of drama was used extensively as teachers exaggerated their expressions and actions to be understood.

Despite their best efforts, the early teachers at Akanksha struggled, with many leaving due to unrelenting pressure. They had come with a belief in a dream, but found that the reality of the everyday challenges was next to impossible to endure. Shaheen's resilience had no boundaries; Akanksha had come to define her life. The sacrifices that the work demanded were difficult to justify for some of the teachers who wanted more balance out of theirs. Shaheen didn't focus on the needs of the teachers; for her it was always about the children. These demands were hard on teachers who desperately needed training, love, and support without which many of them were lost.

Classroom emergencies arose daily. One day, they arrived at school to the Head Sister telling them they would no longer be able to use the classrooms and would have to be taught in the corridors instead. 'What do I tell my children?' Shaheen asked. 'How do I tell them that all these floors of classrooms are lying empty…and that you feel, for no reason, that they do not deserve to use them?' There was the day that the head of another non-profit organization stormed into their classroom saying, 'You've taken our children! We were teaching these children and they've come to you because you have a bus!' Shaheen thought, 'In a community of over ten thousand, should we be fighting over who educates fifteen of them?' Endless instances occurred, from a homeless woman hurling rocks and curses at the children as they walked to school, to Nikki's centre suddenly being taken away, to having to teach her students in a nearby public garden.

Although she was still experimenting on every level, Shaheen recognized the need to expand the number of Akanksha centres. The memory of the bus with a trail of children hanging onto it still compelled her; she had not lost sight of the enormity of the problem in the gratification that came from the small solutions that Akanksha was providing. From Holy Name, the centres expanded to St. Xavier's School, a string of unused rooms loaned by the Indian Navy, and the basement of the Nehru Planetarium. Finding space to teach in continued to be difficult, but each new centre produced more stories to tell to potential investors. Somehow it felt like that momentum was making it, although marginally, easier.

With the number of centres increasing, the team had outgrown the little rented room that had served as their office. The team found they were climbing over boxes of t-shirts and carefully kept artwork done by the children. They already shared the shoebox of a room with Shaheen's friend Abodh, who rescued stray dogs. Eventually they moved the office into her parent's home, where her father would return home from work to a constant stream of volunteers, who were in and out of the family kitchen.

'The pressure was intense. How were we supposed to balance strategy and operations together? Every time Shaheen wanted to go speak to a company for donations, a crisis would arise in the slum. She was trying to sustain Akanksha somehow, making sure buses were reaching on time and that teachers were showing up in centres. There was next to no time to strategically plan out the future. We had to be resourceful in every way. I used an old Boston

Consulting Group template and we managed to craft a five-year plan in order to get our first big donation from the UK. In the little time we had we tried whatever we could to keep our organization breathing.'

—Nandita Dugar, Board of Directors, Akanksha and Teach for India

From the start, Akanksha was not concerned with *trying* to do good, but instead with actually *doing* good things. Shaheen's definition of an excellent education grew with her students, and over the years the team added newer opportunities for the children—sports, mentoring, computers, an empowerment programme, and the performing arts. Art became a central part of Akanksha, providing a platform for creativity, imagination, and free expression. Teachers discovered that students who struggled to express themselves were often able to do so through art. The Akanksha children worked with eminent Indian artists to co-create canvases that were then sold by Christies, an international auction house. They participated in 'Children-for-Children' activities, running art workshops for children from higher-income schools. They created a range of products, learning traditional art forms and adapting them to create peacocks painted on benches, coasters decorated with inspiring words, original canvases, painted wall murals, and diaries interspersed with children's dreams. The Akanksha Christmas and Diwali sales brought thousands of people over the years into a colourful celebration of products.

'As I wandered into their home which was smaller than a twin-size bed, Sunita and Vaishali hurriedly cooked something for me. They pulled out Mehendi cones and started decorating my hands while they navigated the space that was slightly bigger than a bathtub.

'That night, I returned to my home and plumped down on my luxurious queen-sized bed. I just observed everything around me. I asked myself a question that I had never really asked myself before. What had I done to deserve everything that I was blessed with?'

—Ruchika Gupta, Director of Art, Akanksha

The Akanksha Musicals were the next dimension in Akanksha's commitment to the arts. Akanksha brought together professional Directors who worked with the children to produce three Broadway-inspired and adapted musicals. The first was *Operation Khazana*, directed by Indicorps Fellow and Harvard drama student Krishnan. It was an adventure musical where a group of children seeked to find the treasure they needed in order to save their Akanksha centre from closing down. The second, *Once Upon a Time in Shantipur*, was an adaptation of *Fiddler on the Roof* and had at its heart the value of diversity and unity. Shaheen was deeply involved in each musical, from inception to production, writing scripts and lyrics for songs, pulling teams together, and working directly with the children. The third Akanksha musical, *Kabir and the Rangeen Kurta*, remains one of her most important and challenging feats. It was a story of daring to dream and her way of sharing Akanksha's belief in the limitless potential of children. Anand Mahindra, the Chairman of Mahindra and Mahindra, attended the show twice, writing to the children that he'd send 'every pessimist in India to see the show, sure that they would leave filled with hope and enthusiasm for the future after seeing their performance'.

From the beginning, the Akanksha team collected evidence to better understand the impact they were having on children. Detailed observations of every child were scribbled in 'child record' books; daily and weekly assessments were recorded; and parent and student feedback was highly encouraged. They placed a focus not only on how teachers were teaching, but also on whether students were learning.

Shaheen cultivated a strong belief at Akanksha that it was necessary to understand the children's communities. Teachers made frequent visits to the community, following up on children who hadn't come to school, talking to parents about delaying the age of marriage, and listening intently when a family was going through a crisis. Over the years, the Akanksha teachers saw things they could never have been prepared for—incidents of rape and sexual abuse, malnutrition, and disease. They advised pregnant teenagers, appealed to fathers to stop violence at home, and taught children how to stay safe.

Almost every year, massive slum demolitions would raze the community homes or a fire would spread rapidly. Or a health epidemic. Or a tragic accident. Pankaj, a student at Akanksha, died after being hit by a train crossing the tracks a few months after performing in the 'Kabir' musical. These were some of the hardest times at Akanksha, the ones that felt the most helpless, the most futile.

'My name is Seema, and I was one of those average girls from a slum. My Ma married at fifteen, was abused and beaten by my alcoholic father and had the responsibility of raising three children on her own. When I was seven, my father went missing, leaving us in a whirlpool of poverty. My teenage brothers studied until they were twelve, failed, and ultimately dropped out of school. They worked part-time jobs, had virtually no income to bank on; their paths had gone haywire. Ma had no support; there was nothing that could pull her out of her poverty.

'Growing up, I rarely got moments of quality time with Ma as she was always working every minute of the day. Though she could just about feed me, she believed in me, and that was enough. She let me be who I was, and did not force marriage on me. Instead, she sent me to a place where she believed I would learn.

'I somehow found my light in my Rajshree Didi at Akanksha. Unlike my brothers, I had a heroine who believed in me. Even on those days when I wanted to break down in the middle of my chaotic municipal school classes, I knew there was a mentor waiting for me after school, and a mother expecting me when I got back home. Didi made an effort to know Ma, and she met my brothers on multiple occasions. All it takes sometimes for you to believe is meeting a stranger who can grab your child's hand and assure you that he or she believes in your child's potential.'

—Seema Kamble, Akanksha and Teach For India Alumnus and 3.2.1 School Principal

The community was so many things. Cups of steaming tea, children squealing in delight over a white pet mouse, helping to make coconut-filled modaks to place in front of the elephant God at Ganpati. Akanksha teachers watched little girls line up for hours to collect water, babies crawling toward mounds of garbage, and sometimes just wondering how so many things could be so meticulously arranged to fit into a tiny shop. The community was racing through the lanes at night to reach a child who needed to be hospitalized, or holding closely a mother bereft from losing her son, or daughter, while she wept helpless and in despair. It was seeing the stark truth of the dark side of our children's lives juxtaposed against the hope that every parent holds for their children's future as truly as it is their own.

It was the tireless reminder of whom Akanksha was here to help, and what it needed to do.

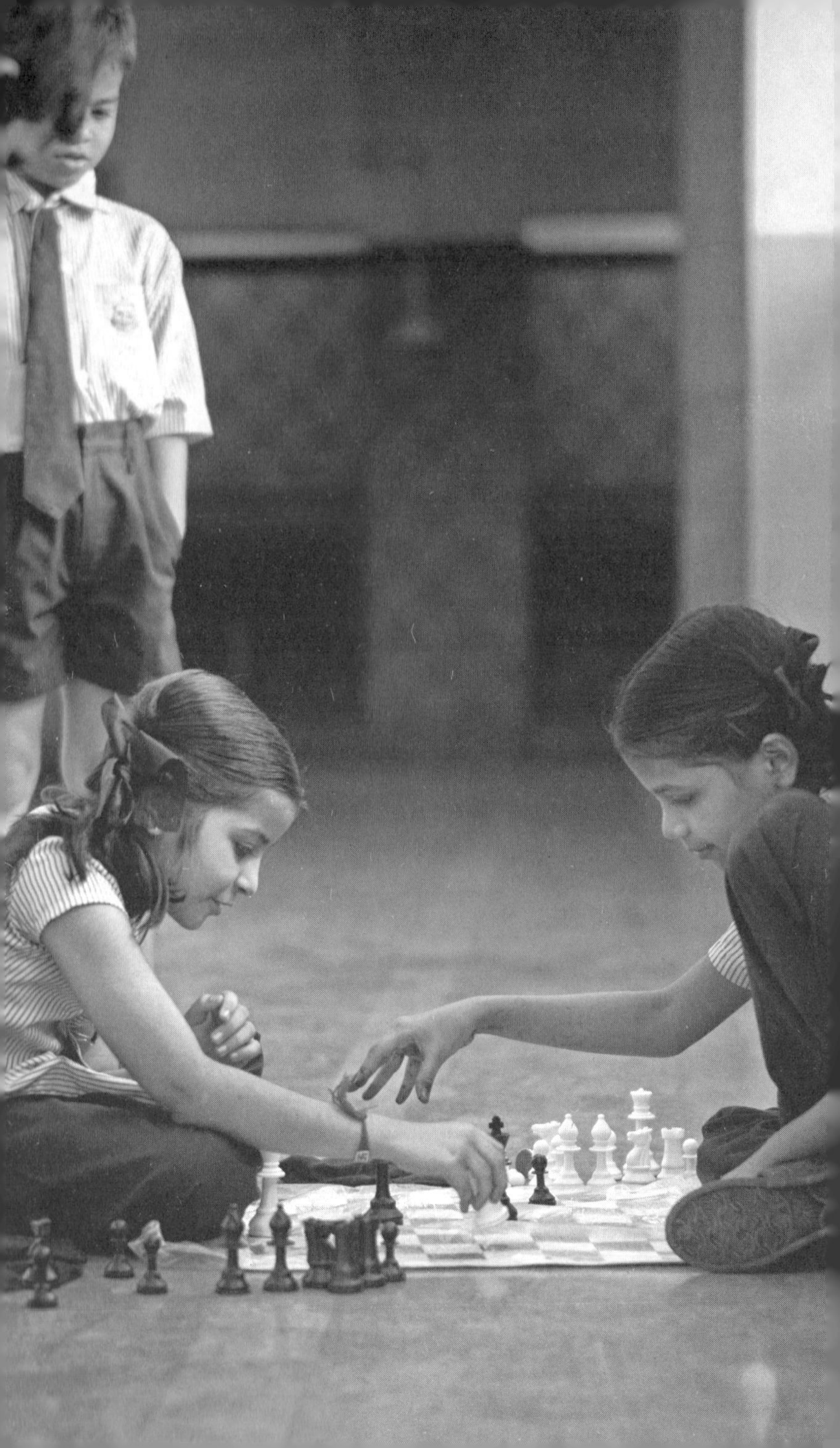

CHAPTER 3

A MORAL IMPERATIVE

'I never feel the power of education more than when I go back to visit the crowded Mumbai slum I started teaching in over twenty years ago. Walking down the maze of narrow alleyways of the slum, I pass tiny home after home. I see girls too young to be pregnant, children who should not have dropped out of school, elderly people ridden with pain due to inadequate healthcare; these are people engaged with the monotonous reality of everyday survival. And then I stop, hearing "Shaheen Didi?" and I see Yasmine, who is now a teacher at an Akanksha School, and married to Sameer, who works at an Information Technology Company. I meet Anu, who is finishing her degree at a leading Mumbai university and Priyanka, who is running a tuition class teaching children in her home to earn extra money for her college tuition. They call me into their homes, chatting in fluent English about their lives, their dreams, and how they are getting there.

'Yasmine, Sameer, Anu, and Priyanka were all students at Akanksha. Today they have sound values, a college education,

meaningful employment. Today they stand on a different life path. I look at them and know that we have a moral imperative to give every child the opportunities they need to maximize their potential.'

Akanksha was now in its 17th year. There was a real office, a clearer vision, and over 200 paid staff members served 4000 children. The model had expanded from a supplemental after-school Centre to an all-day school model. In the after-school Centre, a commitment was made to stay with the children through their schooling years to ensure they got what they needed to be set up for success. Ten years after the Centres were established, Akanksha would work in partnership with the government to run not just Centres, but existing Schools as well.

The 60 Akanksha Centres were places of joyful, holistic learning. Teachers focused on giving their students the ability to work towards and balance three things: their aspirations, achievements, and family reality. As a visitor walking into an Akanksha Centre you'd be hit by a wave of animated chatter, differentiated learning, creative activities, music and dance, conceptual math, and real-life problem solving. You'd see teachers and students share courageously about their lives, guest speakers talk about things ranging from life as a stockbroker to the circumstances that led up to the French revolution. You'd see teachers and students sit on the floor in a circle engaged in an animated discussion on what educational equity means, and children plan a service learning project where they'd choose exactly *how* they would want to make the world better. Everything was about high expectations and the belief was that children would almost always live up to the bar that their teachers set for them.

Outside the centre, students would participate in a range of activities, facilitated either by Akanksha or by one of the many organizations that now partnered with Akanksha. Magic Bus would run sports programmes and Shiamak Davar's dancers would transform classrooms into places of electric energy and expression where dance would be followed by deep discussion about life challenges. Jet Airways took the children on a 'Flight of Fantasy' where the children were welcomed by the ground staff, watched a performance of Bollywood stars at the airport, and were lucky enough to board an hour-long flight with actors Aishwarya Rai and Govinda. As the plane took off, there were sighs of wonder and thunderous clapping. The Akanksha children had access to corporate mentors and would meet them at their offices once a week. Volunteers and mentors spent years, sometimes decades, connected to the children they first met, and to Akanksha.

> *'While we focus a lot on us giving back to the society and kids, one of the most important aspects of being a mentor with Akanksha has been the significant impact it has had on my life. Working with the kids has been an incredibly inspiring experience; their laughter in the face of adversity, belief in a better future for themselves, fighting spirit, religious harmony, ability to derive pleasure from*

the simplest thing, and their maturity beyond their years are more inspiring than anyone can imagine.'

—Sumeet Nagar, Akanksha Mentor and Managing Director, Malabar Investment Advisors

International charter-school models inspired the Akanksha School model where a nonprofit could adopt and run a government school with a high degree of independence, using government resources, while being held to rigorous academic standards. In the Akanksha School model, the government donated the school building, and Akanksha hired the school leader, teachers, and other staff members. Students were chosen by a lottery system and education was provided free of cost.

The Akanksha schools took what the Akanksha Centres had learnt to a whole new level. Unlike in the Centre model, here Akanksha students had the whole day to learn. Students were no longer conflicted by the different styles of teaching coming from their more traditional government schools and the Akanksha Centres. The Akanksha Schools took many of the Centre programmes and adapted them to a full-school model. Students gained a rigorous academic education, focused on developing their character, learnt leadership, practiced service, expressed themselves creatively and worked towards their life goals.

Social workers still spent significant time in the community; school management committees were set up in each school, service learning and the arts were interwoven into the curriculum. Each new school first opened with kindergarten students, and built up one year at a time.

Significant investment was made in training teachers and school leaders in Akanksha values, culture, and pedagogy. The Akanksha Schools committed to giving *all* students broadened life choices, and the results of its first two years of school graduates demonstrated that this was possible. Akanksha's first school to reach the 10th standard had a 100 percent of its students pass the school-leaving state examination two years in a row. Each of these students now had the opportunity to go to college.

In the meanwhile, the population of the community Shaheen had first walked into had mushroomed into tens of thousands of people, and as you walked through the most crowded sections of the community the number of flies seemed to have grown exponentially and they swarmed, sticking to your face and lips. There were more communal taps and a few more tiny toilet cubicles now. There were also more informal drinking dens, and many more cramped shops in a labyrinth of nooks and crannies. Life continued to be difficult, and for many, a drastic struggle for basic survival.

> *'How can I forget the young, frail, single mother of two children who attended my class? Every day I would watch, as she would diligently walk her kids to the bus stop from her tiny home. She had tuberculosis, and even in her pain, I would see a weak smile on her face every time she saw me. "Didi!" she would say. "My pain becomes less when I see you taking them away from me; I know just how happy they are when they learn from you."*
>
> *'A few days later, I went back to the bus stop, waiting for her and her children to arrive as usual. The children were by themselves this time. When I asked them why their*

mother did not accompany them, they told me that she had died that morning. At that moment I realized how much responsibility she had put in my hands before she passed away.'

—Rachna Mathur, former Teacher, Akanksha

Akanksha had intensified its work in the community. A team of dedicated social workers worked with parents. Regular visits to the community made each Akanksha Didi and Bhaiya feel like a rock star, bombarded with smiling children, warm hugs, and generous families. The purpose of community visits was for any and everything—taking a child and parent to the nearest hospital, helping enroll a child in school and supporting families at the time of demolitions. Parents volunteered at the Akanksha Schools and Centres where information on health and child rights was disseminated, and school management committees ensured parent voices were a key part of school decisions. Vandana Goyal, Akanksha's CEO, received a frantic call to the office when a member of the local political party shut down a school after being spoken to in Hindi and not Marathi by an Akanksha staff member. For a week, school remained shut, until a group of parents angrily marched to the Education Minister's office. They demanded the school be reopened. Hours later, the children were back where they belonged. Vandana recalled her reaction afterwards, 'This is what a democracy is supposed to be all about.'

Over the years, Akanksha volunteers and teachers developed a growing network of support that they leveraged in difficult situations. During a slum demolition, Akanksha children and their families were detained in jail so that the police wouldn't experience any 'difficulties' during the demolition. Eventually, Akanksha's police network ensured their release. Twelve-year- old Renuka witnessed her father hurl a large rock at her mother. By the time they reached the hospital, her mother was dead. Her father was arrested and jailed. Overnight, Renuka and her brother Rohit had no family. Within days, Sunil Nayak from the Ra Foundation managed to obtain a scholarship for both children to study at a top tier boarding school. Renuka graduated from class 10 a few years later and went on to study at the renowned Fergusson College in Pune, confident, poised, and having survived the trauma of her childhood.

The Akanksha teachers stretched the boundaries between the lives of their own families and the families of the students they taught. They saw the world as more closely knit than others often do. They learnt from their children.

> *'My student's mothers burned themselves. Their fathers were often drunk and beat up their wives. They were ridiculed for the colour of their skin, often went hungry, and faced the constant pressure of early marriage. Despite that, they would say they didn't need anything when I asked them. They made it through everything.'*
>
> —Anjali Sabnani, former Akanksha Teacher and Director of Education, Akanksha

Shaheen remembers a Sunday at Akanksha teacher Anjali's and Board member Neel's home. Crowded into the guest room were thirty, wide-eyed, happy children watching *The*

Kite Runner. That day was a movie-marathon, with popcorn and lunch. It was really important to Anjali that her children had access to high-quality cinema and that they spent time together, informally These moments were designed to form the foundations of a class that eventually grew into a family.

The Akanksha teachers stood by their children in their darkest times. In one incident, an Akanksha student was raped by her father and stood six months pregnant. Her teacher worked to ensure a safe delivery and the adoption of her baby. Just months after the trauma, she was back in school with another real shot at a meaningful life. When Sumeet, one of our teenage boys, tried to commit suicide multiple times for a complex range of issues—alcoholism at home, low self-esteem, bad grades—his teacher stuck by him until on his third attempt he graduated from school, and set up Pragati, his own non-profit that aimed to bring joy to children in hospitals. When Arif, a precious boy, lost his life crossing the train tracks just days after he completed his 10th standard exam, his teachers and friends sat in the community, in a demonstration of their solemn support for his devastated mother.

Akanksha teachers saw that when class was *meaningful*, children stayed in school. When the P D'Mello road community was demolished and its residents relocated to Mankurd, a ninety-minute commute away, the children still attended school every day, taking a local train to reach. Akanksha teachers recognized that shifting the focus to values changed student's lives. Sangeeta studied at Akanksha, trained as a teacher at the Akanksha Teacher Fellowship, and joined the team managing the Service Learning Programme at Akanksha seven years ago.

'The Service Learning Programme student doesn't take a back seat and crib; he or she does something and is the change. I design sessions and run the operations for the programme; I love what I do and the freedom it gives me to experiment. I am also pursuing a Masters in Elementary Education at the Tata Institute of Social Sciences. I have many dreams. My biggest is to lead a school. I want a good home but I also don't want to run away from my community. It is easy to run away; it's hard to stay there and make the change.'

—Sangeeta Zombade, Akanksha Alumnus and Senior Associate, Service Learning Programme, Akanksha

Akanksha teachers also saw that parents were critical partners in their work with children. After a six-year break from his studies, and after much coaxing, Prashant Dodke appeared for his 10th standard exams. On the night before his last exam, Prashant lost his father. Shaheen rushed to meet his mother, who looked at her blankly and asked quietly if it was okay for her to give Prashant permission to sit for his exam, despite the fact that he was the eldest son and needed at his father's funeral. Prashant's mother worked closely with his teachers over the years to understand the importance of his education, and she knew that this exam was the key to opening choice and possibility for her son. Prashant would say, *'It was only when my results came out and I passed that I felt that she had taken the right decision. Ma feels my whole family's life has changed because of my education. My sister is the first girl in the family to complete her graduation. I take on the responsibility of my whole family. I could not have been a role model for my family without my education.'*

While countless seeds were planted, invisible, along the path where Akanksha journeyed, the Alumni were the most visible manifestation of change. There was Seema Kamble, who after years with Rajshree managed to stay in and finish school.

> 'There were loans, so many loans. I was in the 10th standard, at the peak of academic pressure. Ma was only earning 3,000 Rupees a month, and moneylenders were knocking on our door every day. I tried doing everything I could to earn some money on the side. But sometimes, no matter what you do, everything tears you apart. As I moved into college, I realized I was leading two very different lives: one full of canteen chats and friendly conversations, the other full of poverty and responsibility. The day started at 6 am, when I left my home for college. At noon, I would go to the Akanksha office to earn some part-time money. I would reach home at 7 pm, and conduct tuitions teaching little kids until midnight. When the entire community would go to sleep, I would light a lamp and begin to study for my college classes.
>
> 'As a teenager I used to keep asking myself, "Why me? Why do I always have to sacrifice to make things happen when my friends do not have to? Why don't things get better money-wise?" But my thinking slowly began to evolve. I realized that I had to stop giving myself excuses at some point. Excuses were never acceptable to Shaheen Didi or Rajshree Didi. I could not let my background dictate the way I led my life. And so I stopped. I stopped questioning, and I started answering. I put an end to

giving myself the excuse that I could accept mediocrity only because I led a harsher life than my college classmates.'

—Seema Kamble, Akanksha and Teach For India Alumnus and 3.2.1 School Principal

There was Vanita Kariappa, who was a part of the Akanksha musicals and went on as an Akanksha Alumnus to spread her love for the performing arts.

'I'm interning with Akanksha, writing a book of case studies on our students. I'm studying at Jaihind College. I have started an NGO called Rangmanch, where I teach students from my community the performing arts. I believe in the power of the performing arts. I'm seeing small changes in my kids. Last week, we lost our class space and when I told my kids that class was cancelled that day they didn't agree. They said we'd have class in the garden. One day I will be a teacher. I'm passionate about that.'

—Vanita Kariappa, Akanksha Alumnus and Founder, Rangmanch

There was Jyoti.

Jyoti Reddy's teacher Anjali saw great promise in her and moved her into a private school in the 9th standard, paying her fees to study there. Initially, Jyoti couldn't cope in a system so dramatically different, and she failed twice.

'Anjali Didi kept telling me to keep thinking of the big picture, to not be embarrassed by the fact that I was now so much older than the other children in my class. She was right; if I didn't face this now, what would happen next? Today, I'm in my final year at St. Xavier's College. I want to be a documentary filmmaker. Bollywood films are entertaining but not impactful. I want to make films that have something meaningful to say. It's still hard; I work until 3 am at a call centre and then go to college. But I will get there.'

—Jyoti Reddy, Akanksha Alumnus and Student, St. Xavier's College

In the course of seventeen years, Shaheen realized that achieving Akanksha's mission was *possible*. Irrespective of background, it was possible to work with children to figure out what they needed to transform their lives. Akanksha had now graduated over 1400 Alumni, most of who had taken control of their lives and managed the herculean task of changing their direction.

Every trip to the community, however, was a daily reminder of what would happen if they didn't do more. Bright, talented Feroz took to drugs, joined a gang, and ended up on the street. Meena dropped out of school and ended up on the street as well, pregnant, and ill equipped to raise a child on her own. The social implications of not educating India's children were critical. There was too much terror, sickness, and violence in India for the team not to commit to creating a next generation of children educated to believe in and practice love and peace.

Akanksha knew that its model worked with a high percentage of success, and that it could be replicated. The question now was how to make that possible for *all* children. Shaheen would keep coming back to the memory, now 17-years-old, of how fifteen children boarded that first bus, and how she had no idea how many were left behind. They would hang onto the back of the bus, trying to swing through the door, running after the bus. As the bus left them behind, they stood in the middle of the busy dusty road, horns honking, jumping, arms waving. These children were not numbers they left behind; they were children who mattered. They had the potential to be the next leader in the movement for educational equity, or find perhaps the next cure for a disease, or a solution to the water or energy crisis. Shaheen asked herself what it would take to get every, single child on that bus.

'At the Akanksha schools, we can only admit a select number of students despite the many that want admission. So we use a lottery system; in front of the entire community, we pull names out of a hat. At the end of the day, it's all a matter of luck. Certain students will get to attend our schools while others will have to attend the other schools.

'Every time I have to facilitate this process, I see just how rampant the inequity is around us. Every time I pull a chit, I just know how low the odds are going to be of any given child getting a seat. I see hundreds of families with high hopes who are turned away. I see parents who fight with us, trying to convince us that their children deserve a second chance at the lottery. I see children from the same family having their fate sealed by one draw of

the hat; often one of two siblings will be lucky enough to make it on our list.

'I break down every time this happens. It feels so unfair. What is the fault of these parents after all? Just that they want their children to have a good education, right? It feels so wrong to have this sort of power over their fate. Every child has the right to attend a fantastic school. Why is great schooling a privilege in our country? Why are there so many children and such few opportunities for them to learn?'

—Vandana Goyal , CEO, Akanksha

Shaheen's personal life had also dramatically changed from the time she was a college student at Xavier's. She had married and divorced, and now had a home of her own with her two daughters, Samara and Sana, and several animals. Her daughter Samara attended her first Akanksha meeting when she was a few days old, seated in a booster car seat that Shaheen would carry into meetings. Sana came into their life when Samara was five, bringing boundless energy into their home. The girls grew up living in two worlds. The first was filled with birthday parties, school activities, and travel. Their grandparents played a supportive role in their granddaughters' lives, fostering their interests in music and art, helping them with school, and being ever present for the two girls. This support enabled her to work early and late hours, both in the office and in the community. At the same time, Samara and Sana also grew up in Shaheen's world—attending Akanksha events, visiting the community, making friends with Akanksha children, and doing random acts of kindness on their birthdays.

A few years later, Samara also began assisting a teacher. Across the hall, a class of 40 4th-standard children had no teacher in their classroom, so she stepped in and taught. She would write in her diary when she was 12,

> 'I had holidays so Mama asked me if I could go and help Venil and Thrupti Didi teach in their school. I thought it would be tough and hard, but I thought about those children and how they need to study properly, how they go home to a small house with many brothers and sisters and their mother and father. It must be so tough for them. So I said YES!!
>
> 'After a week of teaching, I leant all their names by heart and they got used to me real quick. I would keep points for the groups in phonics, and correct the Math and English books. All that was very fun for me. Then one day we did a History chapter on the tools of early man. I had some real tools that Nani's friend found in Indonesia, so I took that to show them; they really liked them.
>
> 'I really started liking Aftab and Bashrat. One day, Bashrat didn't come to school for seven days; we did not have a clue why. It was on the 19th of July 2010, he came to school with his mother and he was so thin when I turned around I saw him and my heart beat fast like butterflies flying in my stomach. She told us she was very sorry that he couldn't come to school for so long because he had malaria.'

—Samara Kumar

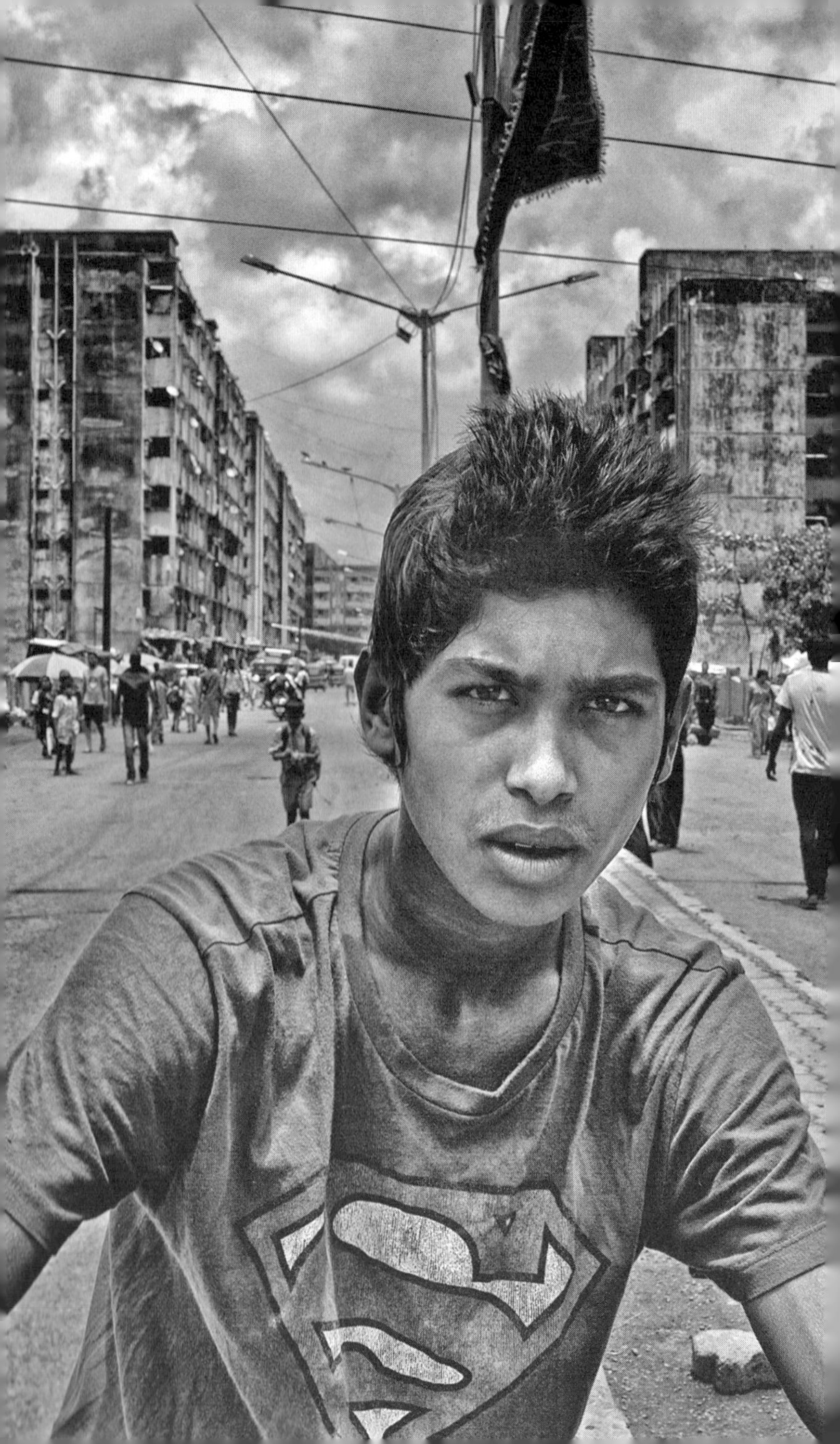

CHAPTER 4

TEACH FOR INDIA IS INEVITABLE

'One day, Shaheen walked into my office and declared, "We have to start Teach for India, and I need your help!" And in my head I thought, why would I ever go to India?

'She kept persisting, and so I finally considered it. I boarded a plane, not knowing where the journey would take me. It was impulsive. I thought I'd just give this a try and see if it actually turned into something.'

—Wendy Kopp, Founder, Teach for America and Co-Founder and CEO, Teach for All

Shaheen discovered that Wendy Kopp had written a book on her Teach For America journey two days before their meeting together. In one day, she read it from cover to cover. Wendy was at Princeton launching the ambitious plan that would become Teach For America in the late 80's at the same time that Shaheen was starting Akanksha. The book *One Day All Children* brought Wendy's incredible journey to life and featured the challenges and inspiration that she encountered when working to place 500 of the nation's best college graduates in America's lowest performing schools for two years.

As a college senior, Wendy had written an unlikely thesis that imagined the creation of a corps of top recent college graduates who would devote two years to teaching in the most challenging public schools. Through that experience they would become lifelong leaders committed to ending educational inequity. Her *'Plan and Argument for the Creation of a National Teacher Corps'* depended on the growing idealism and spirit of service that she believed was inherent in college students. In its first year, Teach For America would inspire thousands of graduating college seniors to apply, and would then select, train, and place 500 Corps Members in schools across the country. This would cost about $2.5 million.

Wendy's team recruited and carefully selected the most committed college graduates from diverse backgrounds to teach for two years. They trained and developed these Corps Members so that they had an immediate and positive impact on their students. They fostered leadership in their Alumni as they addressed the problem of educational equity from all sectors. Each Corps member, Alumnus, and staff member was united by the shared vision that remains boldly printed on Wendy's office: *One Day, All Children in this Nation will have the Opportunity to Attain an Excellent Education.*

~

There was tremendous power in the movement of leaders that Teach For America had built. In 2011 at the 20th Anniversary of Teach For America, an auditorium in Washington D.C. spilled over with more than 11,000 people who had dedicated their lives to ending educational inequity in the US. The country's capital was now filled with Alumni in key positions. The Deputy Mayor of Education was an alumnus. Many of the nation's public schools—and some of its best charter schools—were now being run by Teach for America Alumni. There was a spirit of true revolution in the room: Alumnus Kaya Henderson, now the Chancellor of D.C. Public Schools, boldly declared to a roaring crowd of thousands: 'None of us will be surprised when the woman sitting in the White House is a Teach For America Alumnus.'

Shaheen entered Wendy's office energized, though admittedly tired from a restless night spent awake and reading about Teach For America's journey. She had been struck by the powerful idea that was Teach For America—

that educational inequity was this generation's greatest challenge to surmount, and that thousands of Corps members and Alumni were working relentlessly to solve it.

~

A few months earlier, in a late-night conversation with her close friend Anand Shah, they spoke about the potential of leadership to drive India's progress and its development. Anand and Shaheen discussed a programme similar to America's Peace Corps in India, which would encourage the brightest Indians to focus on the country's greatest problems. For many months, Anand argued that the programme should be broader in scope and encompass challenges in addition to educational inequity. Shaheen, on the other hand, believed in a singular focus on education. She believed that all other inequities were linked to it. In the process of fixing education, everything would change for the better. Anand spoke to her about the Teach For America model that night. Having met four Teach For America Alumni within the past year at Akanksha, she was struck how, despite their diverse teaching experiences in communities across the US, they all spoke the same language around educational inequity and had the same commitment to change it. Shaheen's conversation with Anand had further fuelled her curiosity. What if they could build a movement of leaders committed to the goal of an excellent education for *all* children. How would India change?

When Shaheen first asked Wendy to come to India, she was eager to see if the Teach For America model could work in a very different context. Less than a month after her first meeting with Wendy, she asked again. Wendy said she had shared the idea of visiting India with a few people, who replied that there was still enough for her to focus on in the US. Nevertheless, the idea of Teach For India intrigued her. She would come. A few months later, Wendy landed in India. It was her first trip and she wanted to see everything. Along with Anu Aga, Teach For India's founding board member, Shaheen organized a busy, intense visit.

Shaheen and Anu had met in the late nineties, when Anu was searching for a way to contribute in the field of education. Although her passion at the time was communal harmony, her son, who had always wanted to contribute to education, passed away in 1996, leaving Anu to fulfill his wish. Shaheen and Anu first met at the Willingdon Sports Club where Anu had come with pages of questions about Akanksha. Shaheen left the meeting inspired by Anu's detailed interest in Akanksha's work; similarly, Anu left the meeting inspired by Shaheen's drive for change. That meeting was to become a lifelong partnership and friendship. Anu was to become Akanksha's biggest supporter and spokesperson and the inspiration for Akanksha's operations in Pune.

Anu and Shaheen took Wendy to visit a top-tier college in the city to meet students who could be potential applicants for the Teach For India Fellowship. The three then spent time in a government school, walking past classrooms without teachers, and even where teachers were present, without learning. Wendy, Anu, and Shaheen also met with leaders from India's corporate sector and here Wendy spoke about the power that Teach For India could have to influence the positive development of the country, and the role that the business sector could play in enabling it to become a reality.

> *'I remember a particular moment during Wendy's trip. We were walking down a very crowded street, trying to find the school we were visiting. I remember passing an old man. His feet had open wounds; he was in great pain. I remember stopping to speak with him for a minute, asking if he had seen a doctor, and then walking away with a small part of his pain. Walking out of the school, Anu pulled me aside and said, "I've been thinking about which people I know can fund Teach For India," she said. "I just realized that if I, who believes so deeply in the potential of this idea, don't fund, then who will?" In that moment, on that same crowded road where minutes earlier I had seen that man, she committed five crores. I remember what that meant to me—that only in a place of such inequity could there be such generosity. Anu believed that this was an idea that must happen.'*

As Wendy spoke to hesitant Indian college students, she was reminded of similar doubts from the students in America when Teach For America was poised to launch. It had also been difficult for US School Principals to accept Teach For America's Corps Members, but they had. As she heard corporate leaders in India express their concerns as to whether the country's best and brightest young people would actually apply for the Fellowship, she couldn't help but remember all these same reservations that had since then been dispelled by the successes of the Teach For America Corps Members and students that they had taught back home. Schools desperately needed driven, high-quality teachers. College students everywhere shared an idealism and belief that change was possible. The network to support a movement existed. There was no reason why Teach For India couldn't happen. Wendy left her few days in India with a singular reflection—she was prepared for the differences in context but not fully aware of the vast similarities. Perhaps common challenges could have common solutions.

Anand and Shaheen were joined by a small group of people who began meeting regularly to brainstorm on an idea that would germinate into Teach For India. Most of these meetings resulted in long debates; some broke out into fights. 'Should we start big or with a pilot? Should this be an aspirational programme or one that anyone could join? Should this be a one-year or a two-year Fellowship? Where exactly should we start?'

With many of the debates going round in circles, and tension building between Anand and Shaheen, she went to McKinsey with a request: please help mediate. Over the years, friends at McKinsey had worked to support Akanksha. Their initial response was that they couldn't come in and sort through many debates without a clearly defined client. In Shaheen's view though, this was different. She needed the Teach For India team to work *on* the McKinsey team. They agreed, bringing a diverse and unlikely group of people together to create the Teach For India blueprint. The final group of people included Archana Patel and Anand Shah from Indicorps and Anand Piramal, who along with Anand Shah, had launched the Piramal Fellowship in Rajasthan. Vandana Goyal, who a week earlier had walked into the Akanksha office for an interview for a staff position, was pulled onto the team. Nandita Dugar, a long-time board member of Akanksha and Puja Sondhi, a week-old Teach For America staff member and lawyer by profession, relocated to India. Ashish, Ramya, Ruchi, Vivek and others joined from the McKinsey side.

High above the city at the McKinsey Mumbai office, usually until two or three in the morning, over three months of coffee and a white-board that would miraculously print out what was written on it, the first blueprint for Teach For India was created. The team carefully studied the Teach For America model, the Peace Corps, and others. They looked at the Indian Freedom movement and drew parallels to what Teach For India was attempting to do. They wanted to build something that would change India. Every concern expressed was broken down and debated. Nandita remembers long discussions on how the team would manage to convince parents of young Indian graduates that teaching was worth their time. She remembers discussions on how far outside a city the team would place its Fellows, and what Akanksha's role in Teach For India would be. Akanksha would incubate Teach For India, and, as soon as possible, the organization would spin off as an independent entity.

> 'It was an emotionally charged process. There was so much idealism and passion in the room, and everything was a debate. Should this be a local language programme or an English programme? Should Fellows just teach or grow as leaders? I remember the richness of the debate and how many key decisions about the model started in that room.'
>
> —Vandana Goyal, CEO, Akanksha

At one point Ashish did a session with the team on work-life balance. 'In my fifteen years of working at McKinsey, I've never seen a team work this hard or be as committed,' he said. 'This engagement had such a deep impact on us that all of us on the team deepened our personal long-term commitment to education.' The team interviewed college students and young professionals to see what incentives would entice them to leave what they were doing to join Teach For India. They visited schools to see if teachers with such a different profile than a regular teacher would even be accepted for two-year teaching positions. The debates continued with even more passion, urgency, and energy as time went on. And then, one by one, agreements were reached, and decisions were made.

～

This would be a Fellowship created for the brightest, most committed young people. Teach For India would recruit people it believed had the potential to succeed in the classroom and beyond. The team would ask themselves one question as they were evaluating potential Fellows, 'Do we believe that this person has the potential to be a key leader for educational equity?' Teach For India adapted Teach For America's robust selection rubric, keeping selectivity under 7 percent. The Fellowship needed to be aspirational for young Indians.

This would be a two-year Fellowship. Even though a one-year Fellowship would likely attract significantly more applications, the belief was that Fellows needed an additional year in the classroom to have sufficient impact and leave children with the belief that change was possible. A string of one-year teachers would not be able to have sufficient impact on students.

Teach For India would make a long-term commitment to each child, and would work with a subset of students within a given school until graduation. Ideally, a Teach For India Fellow would start teaching in a second standard classroom. That Fellow would finish his or her Fellowship once the children entered 4th standard, when a new Fellow would take over the class for the 4th and 5th grades. This would continue until 10th standard, when students would graduate from school. This programmatic choice would mean that Teach For India would reach altogether fewer children. It would also mean that Teach for India would have a deeper, more lasting impact on the children it worked with directly.

This was to be more than a two-year teaching Fellowship. Teach For India would be about building a movement of leaders who would *redraw* India. These two years would be critical in fuelling each Fellow's sense of possibility, determination, and belief that equity was attainable; seeing equity being realized in their individual classrooms would give them the faith and skills that they needed to impact a broader scale across India and into the future.

It would start as a two-year Fellowship that would place Fellows in urban, English-medium schools. This was a difficult decision to make, knowing that the greater need in the country was in rural areas and across language mediums. Shaheen believed that it was important for the team to start with what they knew better, and where they could have most visible and immediate impact, and then slowly add complexity to the challenges they took on. Over two decades with Akanksha, she had learnt that English was an important skill for low-income children to acquire in order to get better jobs. Families in the communities where Teach For India launched wanted their children to learn English. They believed that this was an integral part of putting them on a different life path. Teach For India was therefore primed to deliver in English. Additionally, Akanksha had networks and an understanding of low-income communities in Mumbai and Pune, which would be a huge support to Teach For India.

The team realized the need was everywhere. If each child equally deserved an education, they could begin anywhere. And in some ways, disparity was most visible closest to the country's largest urban areas. Children from low-income families in Indian cities lived next door to palatial apartments worth crores of rupees. They attended schools where teachers often didn't show up, where a block away students with high income parents paid lakhs for their children to go to International Baccalaureate schools, in crisp uniforms, sometimes accompanied by their individual nannies in chauffeur-driven cars. Some of India's children played on busy roads, finding any available space no matter how dangerous, while children from high-income schools had access to high-hedged sports clubs with manicured cricket pitches and Olympic-sized swimming pools. To these children Mumbai airport was the gateway to deluxe vacations at Disneyland and other fantastic destinations around the world, while to others the dark narrow winding pathways of the low-income community around the airport *was* the entire world.

The team decided that if they could have impact in these

classrooms, already rife with challenges, then they could use what they had learnt to spread to more challenging areas. Shaheen described those days at the McKinsey office:

> 'All of us were juggling two jobs. Those three months were exhausting and exhilarating. At the end of the three months, we had the answer we had really known all along. Teach For India made sense. It was possible. The only question now was who would make it happen? All of us had jobs that we loved and didn't want to leave. But then there was this hundred-odd page document waiting to come to life.'

When the Teach For India blueprint was ready, the team looked around the table and asked who would take this forward. No one volunteered; everyone had full-time jobs, and there were families, children to consider. Shaheen remembers a text message from Anand. *'Teach For India is Inevitable'*, it said. This was going to happen.

For nearly ten months, Shaheen and Wendy searched for the right person to bring Teach For India to life. They worked with a leading search firm, and the position generated interest, but candidates either seemed to have the professional experience to build a great organization *or* the mission-orientation and passion for children. They needed someone who had both. In the meantime, Mariyam Farooq was sent to India from the brand-new start-up Teach For All, a global network set up to support entrepreneurs around the world who, like Teach For India, believed in this mission.

'We'd review CVs together and put people through a long interview process. A few of them made it to a conversation with Wendy and Anu. And then we got really close to hiring someone; a verbal offer had even been extended. We interviewed the candidate in a full day of meetings and as he left, I remember sitting with Shaheen. She shook her head and said that it wouldn't work. After an 8-month process of looking for people, she knew she had a bigger sense of possibility and more ambitious goals for Teach For India. Her vision was deeper and bigger than anyone else's. Within two hours of that realization, we got on the phone with Anu and Wendy, and let the candidate go. And a few weeks later, Shaheen called me in Pune. She said she had the crazy idea that she needed to do this herself.'

—Mariyam Farooq, Senior Director, Participant and Alumni Impact, Teach For All

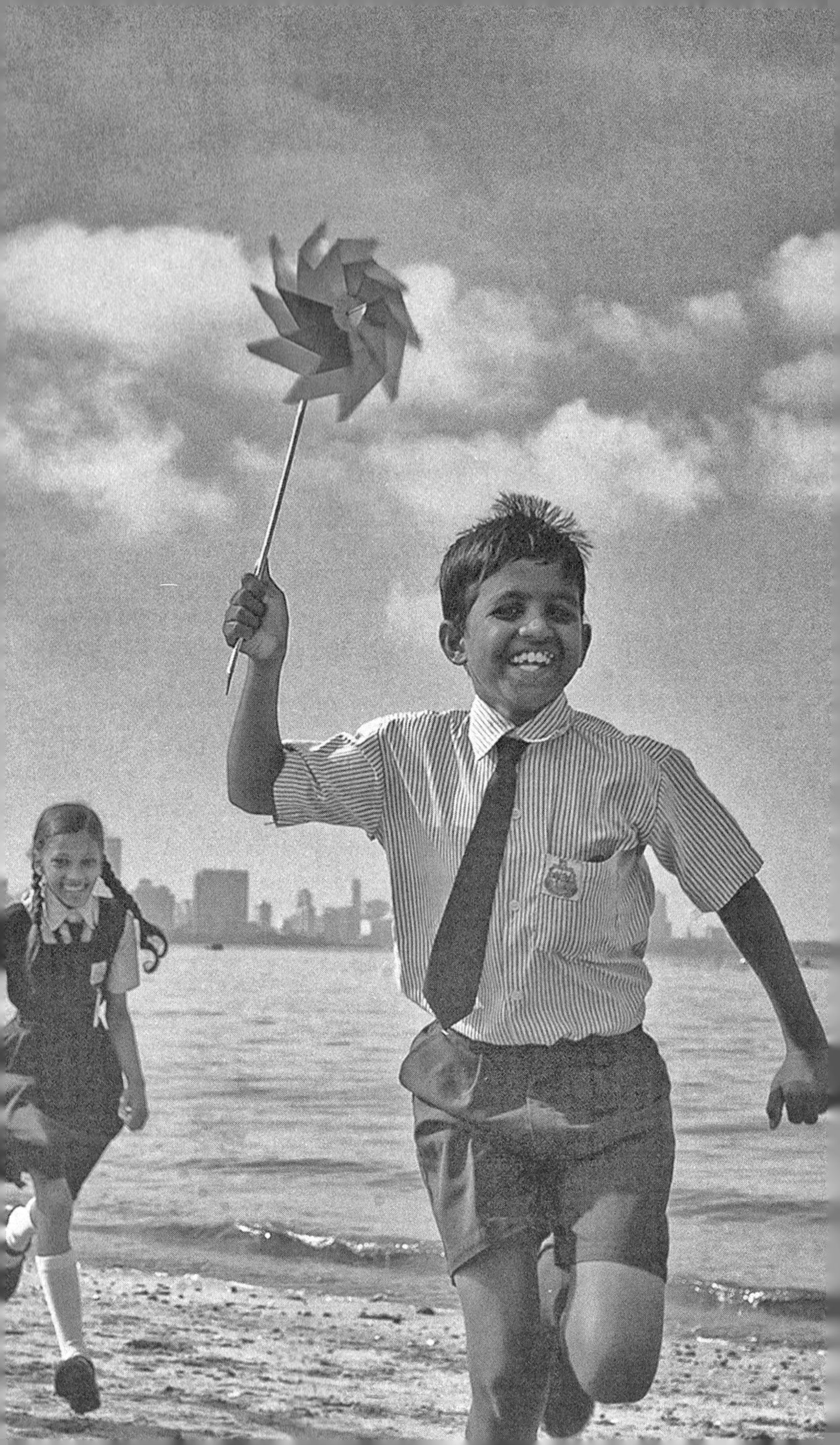

CHAPTER 5

FIRKI

And yet I know that if I wait,
The wind it will be back.
For life it spins a coloured dance,
And twirls along its track.
Here now, it comes,
And round and round.
My Firki runs and runs,
And shows me with great certainty,
A movement has begun.*

---

* From a poem by Shaheen at the Opening Ceremony for incoming Fellows at Teach For India's Training Institute, 2011

In the moments before Teach For India's launch, Shaheen struggled with the question of whether she was the right person to lead it. She understood children, but she knew nothing of building leaders. She worried about maintaining her own joy and energy for her work—working with children directly had always charged her and this job would mean taking one step away from that. After years of working to see change, Akanksha was having impact now; Teach For India would be about long-term impact. At the same time Akanksha had grown organically, slowly, one step at a time and Teach For India would need to leap. She was daunted by the idea of what may happen if they didn't get this right.

> *'I would talk to her about imagination. For me, this was not about whether Teach For India would happen. I knew it would happen and it would happen because of her. It was about what it could really look like. She could deliver on things that just seemed almost impossible to do. She would work relentlessly to make it happen. The sky was the limit.'*
>
> —Anand Shah, Founder, Indicorps

At the same time, fuelled by the interest of several social entrepreneurs across the world, Wendy initiated another study by the McKinsey group based out of New York, to determine the feasibility of a global network of 'Teach For' organizations. Wendy's passion around this particular theory of change expanding internationally was growing. For Wendy, a child in need in her country or in another country was equally valuable. She didn't see broadening the scope as a diversion, but rather thought of it as the continued pursuit of this theory of change. She believed that a unifying model would bring all countries together to strive for educational equity for all children around the world. The issue they were trying to solve was deeply complex and needed leaders around the world pursuing it with equal urgency. Wendy believed that the key to Teach For All's success would be getting the balance of sharing lessons and fostering innovation and adaptation right. She believed that across the world, there was a need to direct as much top talent as possible to this mission. In September of 2007, Teach For All launched at the Clinton Global Initiative with the goal of supporting entrepreneurs in various countries who wanted to build similar movements to Teach For America.

It was through Teach For All that Mariyam Farooq had come to India, becoming Shaheen's right hand and trusted friend in the six months before Teach For India was to launch. Mariyam remembers her Skype interview with Shaheen. 'I was in the US and Shaheen in India. I was dressed in a suit and the Bombay sun shone on her face and made me feel so comfortable. The next thing I knew I packed my bags and moved halfway around the world.'

Mariyam and Shaheen did whatever they could to get Teach For India rolling—they conceptualized the programme design, hired a small team of six people, wrote an initial grant for funding, and visited schools to determine where Teach For India should launch.

Mumbai seemed daunting—complex, large, almost impossible to have an impact in, so Mariyam moved to Pune to test the feasibility of launching Teach For India there. They explored Hyderabad seriously, and other sites, and then decided that with the network Akanksha already had in place, and the fact that eventually they'd certainly need to be in Mumbai, sooner started to seem a better idea than later. With the blueprint serving as a general guide, Shaheen and Mariyam operated largely on instinct as they figured out what needed to be done to be able to launch.

Shaheen started with a focus on Teach For India's vision, mission, and core values. The initial core values generated by the six-member team were Critical Thinking, Reflection, Resourcefulness, Empathy, Respect and Humility, Integrity, and a Sense of Possibility. Empathy would eventually become Seva (Service), and Critical Thinking would grow into the essential value of Excellence. These six core values would continue as an integral part of Teach For India for each year to come. The team talked about two over-arching commitments—the Commitment to Transformation, and the Commitment to Educational Equity. They would try to balance an excellent education in their classrooms with the transformation of themselves, their communities, and consequently, of India itself. Living these commitments was of the utmost importance, and the team continued to push themselves to have experiences that would connect to their children. This would cement and fuel their commitment to Teach For India's mission and values.

> *'Walking through the community, I entered Parveen's home. Over the next two days, I had a bath behind a flimsy cloth curtain that separated two square feet out of the tiny home, and also served as their kitchen. I watched as her mother cooked, in that tiny space, the tastiest Biryani ever, made with so much love. I was amazed as Parveen showed me how her family slept diagonally so that they fit on the ground of their home and then told me with a smile that that is why God made them all short. I watched as Parveen squeezed herself into a pitch-black loft the size of her body to sleep. I marvelled that through the difficulties of poverty but armed with a good education, Parveen had graduated from Sophia College and got a job in Tourism, postponing her engagement by four years so that she would be educated and financially independent when she got married. I sat in that little home watching Parveen do some work on her laptop and waited for her breaks, when she would look up and talk excitedly about her life ahead.'*

~

From the start, Shaheen knew that realizing Teach For India's vision would be entirely dependent on building a driven, skilled team that would live its mission. It was hard to find people in India who shared this particular vision of education, and that wanted to accomplish this ideal with and for low-income students. Early hires came from abroad, mainly from Teach For America and a similar model in the UK, TeachFirst. Srihari Prabhu, an early staff member and Teach For America Alumnus, would say, *'It didn't feel like a national movement. We were six people staffed around one desk. Everyone was involved in everything and we all knew everything that was going on. Every one of us had given up something to be there. For each of us, this was deeply personal.'* Early staff members wore many hats; there was way too much to be done.

> *'The laws that governed those first two months were insane, like the entire universe was working against you and then at the last minute, the laws were suspended, and you were reminded of the sense of hope. I worked on recruitment, and two weeks before our first deadline, we were in crisis mode. Our goal was 1000 applications; we had 600. And then, hours before the deadline, we saw the numbers rise from 600 to 1300. A few days after I started working on recruitment, Shaheen walked up to me and said, "How would you like to help design our first Training Institute?" Confident as I was at 22, I said yes. The next months were crazy. People laughed when I said our Institute day should go from 7 am to 8 pm, and our main Institute trainer pulled out weeks before Institute. Again, the laws of the universe suspended. We found amazing trainers in Ben and Ambler from Teach For America and pulled off a really beautiful Institute. On the last day at Closing Ceremony, I remember looking on stage, seeing our 87 Fellows about to leave to meet the*

kids in their city classrooms, feeling like something just happened that was about to make history.'

—Sandeep Rai, former Teach For America Alumnus and Pune City Director, Teach For India

The first major challenge the team faced was finding schools where Fellows would teach. After unsuccessfully trying to design an organized system for the school placement search, the team literally walked into communities, started talking to children in school uniforms, and asked for the nearest school. They'd often walk past schools in the community, hidden among hundreds of other tiny, tin-roofed rooms. School visits were a combination of cups of tea, sharing a Teach For India brochure, and tactfully asking head masters for permission for Fellows to teach their children. Finding high need schools that also met basic standards necessary for success—classrooms, blackboards, bathrooms—was immensely challenging.

'One day, Shaheen and I decided to just go out into the street and find schools. We had no idea of how to do this. We asked people on the street where the schools were, and slowly a group of five kids that were just following us around started taking us to school after school. Sometimes in ten minutes of walking, we'd find ten schools. We wanted to choose schools that were challenging, but we weren't sure of just how challenging. Some schools had tin roofs, no fans, were cramped and completely unsafe. One school we passed by was in a noisy factory warehouse, and the 80 children and

teacher needed to pull down the heavy shutter to block out the noise.'

—Garima Kapila, former Mumbai City Director, Teach For India and Head of Operations, Swasth

School Principals and staff were concerned about the relatively young age of Teach For India Fellows, and their lack of teaching experience. Many of the teachers in these schools held Bachelor of Education degrees, and they were unsure whether Fellows would adhere to and complete their school curriculum. Teach For India was careful to place Fellows only where the school had a teacher vacancy, so that no existing teacher was displaced from a job. They also negotiated a long-term commitment with the school so that Fellows could be placed with the same set of children right until graduation.

Given the diversity and complexity of the schools, the Teach For India team had ongoing debates on how to best measure the impact of Teach For India on students. Ninety percent of the classrooms had children who would test at pre-kindergarten levels. Unsure of how to set ambitious yet feasible goals for students, they borrowed an idea from Teach For America: *1.5 years of growth*. To get students to grade level and not give Fellows an impossible task, a year and a half of growth in one academic year seemed significant and possible. A year in, they would realize that other classrooms in the same school were often making one fifth of this growth, and 1.5 years was an extremely formidable goal.

The next challenge was to ensure Fellows accepted Teach For India offers to teach in these schools. In India career and life choices were largely family decisions, and the team was now faced with the question of whether or not the strongest young people—those with the *most* number of career options—would actually choose the two-year-long Teach For India Fellowship.

> 'We were clear that we needed the most driven people to get into education. Our theory was that if we get the best people, education would change. So we wanted to start small, with 100 Fellows. We weren't ready to take on more.'
>
> —Sheela Prasad, former Teach For India staff member and Cluster Partner, Teach For America

Shaheen's greatest fear was that Teach For India would attract the most idealistic and capable people, but not be able to support them to be successful teachers. What if Teach For India was not able to create an experience that grew each Fellow's sense of possibility? What if Fellows stopped believing that the problem was solvable? These were precious people, a very small and capable minority who were willing to stand up against popular opinion and choose the road less travelled. If Teach For India wasn't successful, it actually ran the risk of *compounding* the problem it was trying to solve.

~

With close to no money to allocate to building a brand, the team set out to create a credible, inspiring, and nationwide identity. Although Teach For India would launch in just two sites, they wanted the first 100 Fellows to come from every part of the country. Designer Rabia Gupta created a logo around the idea of an India—literally, redrawn. The team started using important phrases that would become a part of Teach For India language: *Redraw India, Are You Ready for a Challenge, Join the Movement*. Children and leadership were at the centre of the Teach For India brand, which always included a call to action. One of Teach For India's favourite early posters compared 'settling' in an office with changing lives in a classroom. The best way to attract the country's most motivated people was to speak their language.

> 'Our posters that year could only speak of the idea—we had no Fellows and no testimonials. We were just selling an idea we believed in. We asked people if they wanted to "settle", or "choose to fight". We knew this was a big risk for people, and so knew that our inspiration had to be greater than the risk that was Teach For India itself. We needed visionaries. We needed idealists: the crazy ones.'

—Somika Basu, former Director of Communications, Teach For India

Shaheen knew that the media could make Teach For India aspirational and so, in 2008, she walked into the office of Jaideep Bose, the *Times of India*'s Chief Editor. Not dissimilar to the impassioned plea she made years earlier to get her first Akanksha space, Shaheen painted a picture of what Teach For India could be for India's children. Jo Jo, as she soon called him, instantly connected with this idea. He was a believer in education and in the power of the media in creating a better society. Over the next few weeks, they worked closely to design striking ads that asked for the 'Best Minds and Biggest Hearts'. The *Times of India* ran regular, large ads for Teach For India free of cost in the upcoming weeks. When Teach For India was about to launch, they designed a four-page spread on the idea, which was responsible for giving Teach For India 80 percent of its first Fellow cohort. In the years to come, Shaheen would often remind Jo Jo that his belief and the support of the *Times of India* had been instrumental to the existence of Teach For India.

~

Convincing schools to let Fellows teach was difficult but persuading colleges to allow Teach For India to present in their classrooms was an even bigger challenge. Teach For India posters would say,

> *You could settle. For the designation. The Neat Paycheck. A Boss. A Schedule. Your Dad's profession. Your Mom's approval. Or you could fight. For that Dream you've always had. For a Changed Nation. For a hundred kids you don't even know. For their Freedom. And your Freedom. For the Leaders they could become. And the Leader you know you can be.*

College Principals sometimes supported Teach For India, but often were skeptical about whether their students would be interested in the Fellowship and if Teach For India would build the leadership qualities necessary for a wide range of jobs. 'What will our students *do* after teaching for two years? Why will any other sector hire them?' they would ask. Rebecca Noecker, one of Teach For India's early employees from the US, recalls Teach For India being a 'hard sell'; people would ask how they'd be able to support their families if they took a step like this. One potential applicant told her that the programme didn't seem genuine. 'I was too polished and the programme was too good to be true.' When the Teach For India team were given time to present, they brought Teach For India's vision to life. The presentation would showcase an Akanksha student, Jyoti. Her speech at TEDx was a powerful, living example of change, after which the audience would be engaged in a simulation of educational inequity that mirrored the reality of India: 10 percent of the room represented the number of Indian children who actually go on to college. Before the audience left, everyone sang together.

Regardless of the difficulties, Shaheen found spirited students who would comprise her first Fellows from colleges and organizations across India. Twenty-one-year-old Anasuya Menon remembers trying to skip class the day when her Principal forced her into the Teach For India presentation. Anasuya was struck by Shaheen's words on inequity in the country; many of her classmates however were uninterested.

> *'The few of us who applied had no idea if this would help us grow or if it would be bogus. But we had faith in the belief that Shaheen had. Many of us were angry by the Mumbai bomb blasts. We were fuelled by this crazy idealism and a utopian dream for our country.'*

Fellows had to tackle their own doubts about the movement and deal with resistance around them. Manu Jindal remembers his extended family members being shocked by his decision to become a Fellow. 'You are an engineer working in corporate strategy; you have done an entire summer programme in Chicago. And now you want to be a primary school teacher in a slum?' they would ask in confusion. Aniket Thukral, the last Fellow to join the Fellowship in the first cohort, would struggle for months to explain to his family the value he would find in teaching low-income children. Even though his parents were ironically both teachers, it would take time before he would be able to 'align their hopes and dreams' with those of his own. Shantanu Bhattacharya, Teach For India's Recruitment Manager, presented to more than 20,000 students around the nation.

> 'One day, a student dressed in a burkha walked up to me after my presentation and said that her mother and grandmother at home had to dress like that as well. She said by being a Fellow this was the cycle that she was going to break.'

While the team was travelling around the country recruiting young people, they were simultaneously running a rigorous selection process. Based on their written applications, candidates were invited to assessment centres, where they completed sample-teaching lessons, participated in an in-depth one-on-one interview, and co-led a group discussion.

> 'We'd spend a full day with each Fellow in borrowed corporate space for the assessment centres. We'd look at

a range of hard and soft competencies to evaluate fit into our programme. And then, we'd have a chart up in our little office in Pune and as Fellows accepted our offers, we'd list them up on the chart. Every time a name was added, a cheer would go up in that little office.'

—Kavita Rajagopalan, former staff member, Teach For India and Programme Head, Villgro Innovations Foundation

~

In May 2009, 87 Fellows would start teaching 3000 children across 34 schools. Shaheen knew that the Fellows would struggle; a huge amount of thought and effort needed to go into the love, support, and development of each of them. Planning the first training institute was a challenge. The team hadn't recruited a Training Director, and most of them had never seen one of Teach For America's training institutes. They learnt wherever they could, from within India and internationally, to create a five-week residential induction that would both prepare Fellows to be strong beginning teachers and also induct them into the culture and values of Teach For India's vision.

While much of those first few months were focused on the programme—finding Fellows and schools and figuring out how to prepare them for day one of school—there was also the chaotic frenzy associated with a start-up organization.

'We were running around getting people to believe. We met donors in hotel lobbies as we looked for an office, and covered the walls of my house with chart-paper to design our organizational charts. Funds were not coming through, there were daily fires to put out on the school placement side, and the incorporation of Teach For India was a nightmare. After a ridiculous amount of back and forth with a government office in Mumbai where things kept getting delayed in our registration process, someone called to tell Shaheen that they should just make a payment and get the situation resolved. I remember Shaheen calmly excusing herself from the room and going to a quiet place. I could hear her, sternly but gently, saying "That is not who we are. That is not what we do." I understood at that time what Teach For India was all about.

'We would hear no after no after no. And then there was a point where we picked momentum. The Pune Commissioner showed incredible excitement in what we were doing. I remember him saying to Anu and me, "Give me these people right now!" His energy was what we needed; it made everything possible. After that, things started happening. We got our registration done, posted our first job descriptions, and saw excitement turn into funding.'

— Mariyam Farooq, Teach For America Alumnus and Senior Director of Participant and Programme Impact, Teach For All

Three days before Teach For India's first-ever cohort was to enter training, Shaheen realized that they needed a symbol, something that stood for children and for change. As she drove past there was a man selling Firkis on Chowpatty beach. A hundred pinwheels turned in the wind. Nearby, children ran, their Firkis spinning in the wind. *'That's it!'* she thought, *'It keeps the child at the centre. Its colours remind us that this is a journey of finding our colours as we help our children find theirs. And when it spins, it is symbolic of a movement.'*

Three days later, at Teach For India's first opening ceremony, the first 87 Fellows would be welcomed with tears, laughter, and hope as they stepped together onto the stage, while the Teach For India team handed each one of them a Firki.

The Firki would become the symbol for Teach For India—spinning discovered colours to form a movement.

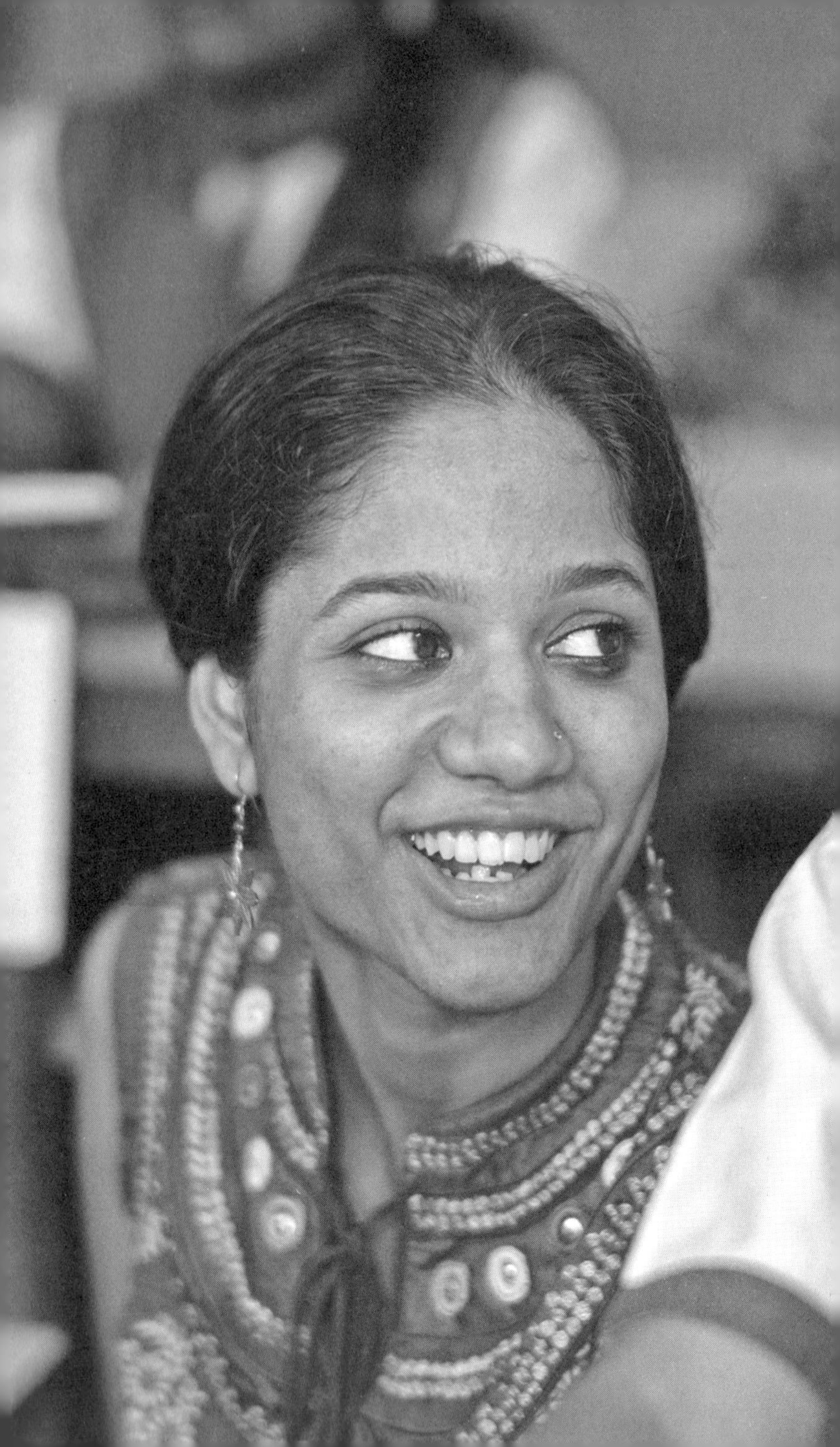

CHAPTER 6

THE NINERS

'In my dreams I have seen magical tales of a glorious country, heard wonderful stories of prosperous people, and witnessed mesmerizing spectacles of a nation at its zenith. I now want to sketch my dreams on the canvas of real life.'

– Gaurav Singh, 2009 Teach For India Alumnus and
Founder, 3.2.1 Schools

Shaheen met Gaurav in the cafeteria of the Symbiosis College in Pune on the first day of Teach For India's Institute in 2009. He told her he had goosebumps being there in that moment, and when she looked at him quizzically, he pointed down to his arm to show her. He *did* have goosebumps, and proceeded to tell her the story of how he came to Teach For India.

'I was working for Accenture, and had to take a mock CAT exam. I had procrastinated to the last possible day until I had to finally start studying. I got home late with food poisoning and vomited all night. There was nobody with me. By the end of the second day, some friends came over to give me medicine, and after a few days, still sick, I went home to Lucknow. The day before I was supposed to fly out to take my exam, the fever kicked in again. Not able to sleep, I picked up a copy of the Times of India *that my friend had left in the apartment. I read the line "We ask you to Teach For India for two years". I didn't see the "Teach", only the "India". I went straight to the website and in exactly three seconds, I knew I'd do it. My friends attributed that decision to the fever. I didn't. I had always wanted India to be the Golden Bird*

it had once been known as. And now I had the chance.'

—Gaurav Singh, 2009 Teach For India Alumnus and Founder, 3.2.1 Schools

Each of the 'Niners,' as the Class of 2009 was commonly called, had their own story of what had brought them to Teach For India. Madhumita Subramanian returned from the UK to the challenge of working on the ground in India. Charag Krishnan was working at Bharat Petroleum and planned to do a degree in Electronics abroad when he saw the advertisement for Teach For India. He researched both Teach For America and Teach For India before deciding he wanted to teach. Anirrban Mukherji was Xavier's top-ranked student that year and had an attractive job offer at Maruti Suzuki. When he heard about Teach For India, he decided that at Maruti he would be replaceable, but Teach For India needed him.

Sana Gabula had spent the past two years at General Electric and was poised to join an internal leadership development programme, but her conversations with children selling books at the traffic light changed all that. She saw how the system was failing them. She learnt about Teach For India and applied.

Romana Sheikh was in her final year of college, a prime candidate for a high-level job in finance, when the 26/11 terrorists attacked Mumbai. As a Muslim, she was especially shaken; her ideas of security and safety were all of a sudden called into question. A few months later everything seemed like it had returned to normal, but Romana still couldn't understand. She didn't *want* her life to go back to normal. Teach For India was her way of finding a group of people willing to take on the challenge of building India's future.

Shrutika Jadhav had just finished her MBA and was working with ICICI. Like Romana, she too was deeply shattered by the terrorist attacks and searched for a way to contribute.

'When the Mumbai attacks happened, I felt helpless. Everyone around me went back to his or her normal lives, but I just couldn't. Perhaps I was the crazy one. I quit my job and sat at home. There were passive aggressive arguments with my parents over dinner, night after night. "You have an education loan to pay off. You are wasting years of hard work. How will you get married like this?"

'I understood where they were coming from, but my heart kept telling me to wait for something that I would fit into, and to not listen to my head. My head was telling me that if my boss offered me my job back, then I should join again. But then I got my acceptance letter from Teach For India — a movement that was just about to be born. I went back to my boss who looked at me with joy. I remember his words "You are getting a chance that I never got. If nothing else — do this for yourself." I realized that I needed to be the change, and I gave it my all for the next two years of my life. I wasn't sure this was the right decision for me. That is, until I got to Teach For India's training Institute.'

— Shrutika Jadhav, 2009 Teach For India Alumnus and former Teach For India staff member, Programme Manager at the Indian School Leadership Institute

The Niners had to overcome personal and professional obstacles to even reach the first day of the Fellowship. Gaurav's mother was aghast, and his boss called him an idiot. It actually cost him money to leave his company. Manu Jindal's family told him he was creating a fantastical world. They believed an MBA would be necessary for him to join the family business. Charag's family similarly thought he was crazy.

Gaining admission into Teach For India was a challenge of its own. A lengthy online application and essay questions forced applicants into real reflection on who they were and what they wanted, both for themselves, and for the future of India. A phone interview was followed by a full day Assessment Centre, where applicants went through a rigorous in-person selection process.

> 'We will have to make sure that we fight the demons that lunge at our every dream, that extinguish our every hope, and that cripple our every endeavour. To do all this we will have to give our nation a form, a shape, a body. A body which can grow faster than the despair of the poor, be stronger than the fears of the weak, grip tighter than the stranglehold of illiteracy, think faster than the scheming corrupt, and endure much more than what adversity can offer. They say "one day" India will become a superpower. Who are these "they" who say what they say, but always only "say?" When will that "one day" come? In the next century, generation, or decade?'
>
> —from the application of Gaurav Singh

On May 4th, 2009, the Niners received their anxiously anticipated acceptance emails, which said that Teach For India was 'honoured and thrilled to offer them a place in the 2009 batch of the Teach For India Fellowship', and that 'the experience of the inaugural batch of Fellows would determine the course of this movement to end educational inequity for years to come'. Acceptance letters in hand, and families mostly still unconvinced, the Niners entered Teach For India's first-ever training Institute.

~

Institute was designed as a five week, residential experience that aimed to make each Fellow a strong beginning teacher while inducting them into Teach For India's vision, culture, and core values. Although the movement was in its pilot year, only 7 percent of applicants to the Fellowship were selected, the ones that Teach for India believed were the very best that the country had to offer. Shveta Raina, Marketing and Recruitment Director at the time, remembers waiting at the desk of Symbiosis.

> *'I just sat there, praying that our Fellows would show up. Then they started coming in. Many came with their parents and extended family members who were unsure about who exactly they were about to leave their sons and daughters with.'*

The first Fellows came in feeling all kinds of things— nervous, confused, excited, confident, scared. Shrutika was overwhelmed by the warm and professional welcome.

Aniket wondered whether he had joined a cult of idealism. Anirrban was struck by the diversity of the cohort. Gaurav rushed into the washroom after the first hour to cry. It was a breakdown rooted in the knowledge that he wasn't alone. He remembers that moment vividly,

> 'All my life I thought I was the weird one—until I came to Institute that is. I looked around the auditorium that day and asked myself, "Where have you people been all these years?" I knew right at that moment, that there was no way I was returning to my old world.'

Opening ceremony was beautiful. Each Fellow was welcomed onto the stage with a Firki. For days after that one could see the Firkis that Fellows had gifted to children all over the community spin on little chai stalls in the lane outside the Institute.

The first three days of Institute included Teach For India's 'Induction', which had nothing to do with teaching. Fellows spent the first day examining an orange in the greatest detail—smelling, observing, tasting, and even listening to it. This was an exercise in learning; to learn to look at an everyday object in a completely new and different way. The Fellows then entered a community to 'connect' with a child. 'Remember the orange,' they were told. 'Look at your experience in a whole new way.' They spent the second day living one of Teach For India's core values, a Sense of Possibility. They met Akanksha students and Alumni who were in college, confidently sharing the many highs and lows of their journeys. The Akanksha children gave the Niners advice: get to really know and love your kids, make class joyful, and *never* give up.

Fellows were asked to perform impossible tasks like feed a hundred people without any money, make something beautiful from garbage, or simply perform random acts of kindness — all wearing the signature 'Yellow Hat', symbolizing possibility. There was only one rule. The Fellows were not permitted to refuse any challenge, instead they were encouraged to be open to the possibility of perseverance, to say 'I *can*'. On the third day, Fellows shared their personal life stories with each other in an exercise termed 'life maps' that went on for many hours. Seated in a circle, with people who had been strangers only three days before, they spoke not only of the exhilarating successes of their lives but also of their darkest, most private pitfalls. They shared about abuse that they had endured, deep insecurities they had, and confessed to the serious mistakes that they had made in their lives. The group held each experience without judgement in a safe space. Sessions lasted for six hours and built deep trust. As a consequence, many of the Fellows and staff made close and lasting friendships. Induction was a rollercoaster of emotions that pushed many Fellows far beyond the limits of their comfort zone.

For five weeks they took the slow and sometimes painful, but often joyous steps to becoming a teacher. The first Institute was framed around Teach For America's 'Teaching as Leadership' principles. The premise was simple and powerful: all great teachers and great leaders applied the same six principles to have significant impact. They set an ambitious vision and goals, invested others in that vision, planned purposefully, executed effectively, and worked relentlessly to continuously to improve their effectiveness.

At the Institute, they would learn these principles in sessions and practice them while teaching in summer school. All sessions and activities during Institute would be about learning and living these principles. This kind of intensive coaching and support would not stop at the end of five weeks, but continue through the two years of the Fellowship.

Shrutika returned furious after her first day of summer school. She had seen the statistics, had read Teach For India's recruitment message 'Are you ready for a challenge?', but had no idea the extent to which the system was failing children until she met them on that first day. 'It's not going to be possible,' she said. 'What we are trying to do is too difficult!' The children in her class were years behind where they should have been in every way imaginable, and she had so little time with them.

The core of the Institute was summer school, where in small groups, closely supervised, Fellows made their first lesson plans and taught their first classes. Aniket Thukral remembers trying everything possible to get little Supriya to listen, while Supriya just wanted to dance, and twirled incessantly to see her skirt go around and around. Sanaya Bharucha began what would become common practice in her classroom through her two years—songs for every concept. Abhik Bhatacharjee would transform his class into a party, where students had to calculate party budgets learning math, figure out whom they wanted to take to the party learning values, and choose anywhere in the world to visit, while learning geography. Classes were often boisterous and difficult to manage, and lesson planning was tedious and complex, but the campus was alive through most of the night with staff and Fellows working and learning together, one step at a time. It was common to walk into the mess hall at 3 am and see Fellows engaged in a debate about children, or a group of people sitting with charts and sketch pens making teaching aids for tomorrow's class, or to hear a Fellow complaining he couldn't draw and witness another Fellow step in to help.

After summer school each day, Fellows would attend culture, content, and pedagogy sessions. One session would introduce them to teaching Language or Math. Another pushed them to examine the biases that, unbeknownst to even themselves, would undoubtedly carry over into their work if not addressed. In sessions they would analyse data, learn the skill of backwards planning, dive into the meaning of the core value of Respect, and play out every thinkable situation in preparation for what they would encounter in the classroom. They quickly picked up a whole new dictionary of abbreviation: GP (guided practice), INM (introduction to new material), PM (Programme Manager), TT (transformational teaching) and many others. Session facilitators would call classes to attention by shouting out 'One team!' and the class would respond 'One mission!' Evenings would consist of meetings for staff member support, lesson-planning clinics, and workshops by experienced educators. Leaders from across sectors were asked to share their learning with Fellows. Actor Aamir Khan visited the Institute, inspiring Fellows as he shared his leadership journey. Madhumita Subramanium remembers being numb for days after social activist Vipin Thekkekalathil spoke to Fellows about child abuse.

A key session at Institute was the Alumni, or 'puzzle' session, where Fellows were introduced to the idea of the 'puzzle of educational inequity'. During a conversation with some of her early staff members at the Institute, Shaheen had asked them what problems they thought would need to be solved in order for Teach For India to accomplish its mission. The team decided to turn over the question to the Niners, who were then asked where the gaps were, and what pieces they would need to fill them. Together, they began to identify the pieces, both within and outside education, that leaders would need to impact to attain educational equity. Some of these were within education: teacher training, curriculum, and school leadership. Others were outside education: business, media, and politics. The puzzle was symbolic of two things. On the one hand, it represented the number of areas to be impacted for educational equity to be solved. On the other, individually the pieces were nothing; the puzzle only made the picture if the pieces fit together. That first puzzle session served to lay the foundation for increasing deliberation around what it would take to get to Teach For India's vision over the years to come.

The small staff team told Fellows that they were learning alongside them. Much had been borrowed from Teach For America, without staff really knowing how to adapt it to an Indian context. Many staff members had limited experience in teaching, and many of them did not know much about India. Additionally having a cohort so diverse came with its own challenges. Coming from radically different backgrounds and lifestyles, Fellows often questioned each other's choices, and even their abilities to speak the English language. Open forums as a result were started where Fellows and staff could share anything with each other. Relationships were central to everything, and staff members were there at all hours, for anything at all. Days were long and stretched to their limits, often too intense for many Fellows. And then there was this overriding feeling that could only be so simply put; there was joy.

> *'I won't ever forget the first rain. I think it was week two or three at the Institute when we heard it. We were all in sessions. Suddenly, everyone ran out into the rain. There was a grassy hill outside and the Fellows started rolling down the hill, covered in mud, laughing in the rain. There was an electricity, such energy and pure joy in that moment.'*

Anasuya describes that first Institute as 'the purity of idealism, the strength of our vision, the clarity of intention, the magic of acceptance in diversity'. For her, Teach For India's first summer institute was a kaleidoscope of possibility. It was the birth of a movement and the start of a journey that would change their lives forever.

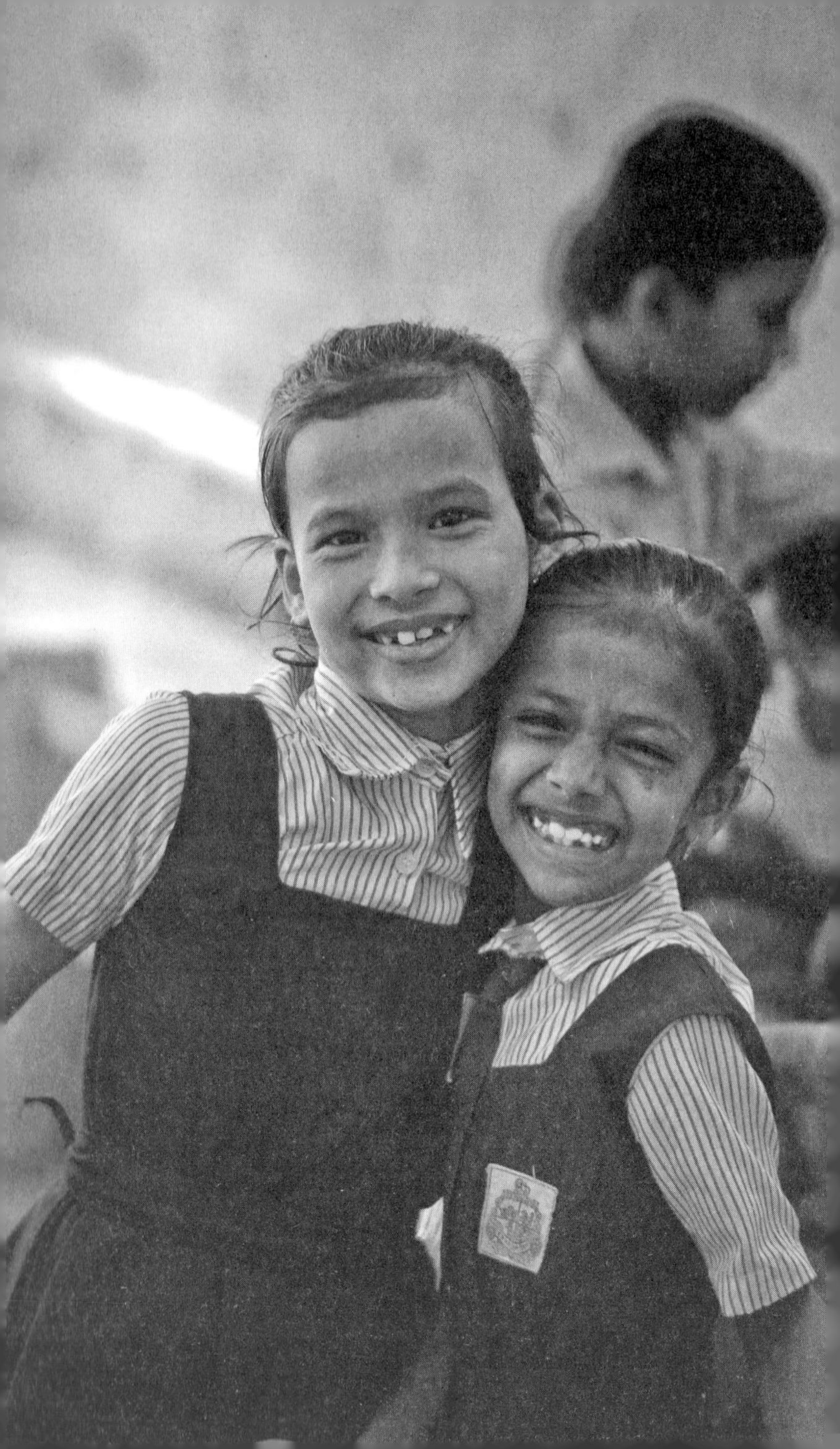

CHAPTER 7

THE FIRST YEAR

The best teachers dream.
Dream big,
Dream new,
Dream of what each child can do.
And see,
And love,
And hate,
And change,
A new world.
They say,
Re-arrange it.
Make it,
What and how you wish,
A goldfish in a square-ish dish.
A forest that keeps growing tall,
A world where we respect the small.
A world where no one goes to war,
Where every single child's adored.
Where no one sleeps,
On sun-baked streets.

Where people smile,
When people meet.
These teachers they teach,
How to fish.
And when to ask,
And what to wish.
And how to do,
The things you fear.
And how to question what you hear.
They teach you how a colour feels.
And to ask why,
And not to steal.
And why the sun goes down at night,
And that to cry is quite alright.
They set a vision for their class,
Plan each detail of their plan.
Reach out to every single child,
Until each one says yes I can.
I know I can,
I must,
I see.
I do believe,
I can achieve.
The world can be,
The world I see.
You Fellows came, courageously,
You Fellows learnt, relentlessly.
And through the challenge of these days,
You learn to try a thousand ways.
To take a breath and set a goal,
So big it stirs your very soul.

And then, in this, each child invest,
I can. I will. This is our test.
To backwards plan from end of year,
To each objective now and here.
To unpack standards, and to map,
Each book and topic, find the gaps.
You learn to chant, you learn to sing,
That art can teach you anything.
You balance both your head and heart,
You learn to stop, reflect, re-start.
You learn non-stop because you see,
Our mission's deepest urgency.
Starts not with them, or he, or she,
The strange thing is,
This starts with me.
Not he, or she,
But me, yes me.
And all together,
We, yes we,
All of us,
Must learn to lead,
To understand what India needs.
For all of us,
Are in this fight,
To make things for each child more right.
To make things for each child more right.*

---

*From Shaheen's Speech at the Opening Ceremony to the first cohort in 2009

'I stand under a leaking roof in a classroom without electricity or proper ventilation, trying to explain place values to my 2nd graders. There are times when I'm overwhelmed, frustrated, tired, and completely zapped. When that happens, I could stand there and complain about everything that's going wrong or I could draw inspiration from the 44 kids who trust me enough to trudge through muddy waters to come and see me try my best at teaching them.'

—Madhumita Subramanium, 2009 Teach For India Alumnus, ED.M in Mind, Brain and Education from the Harvard Graduate School of Education, and Assistant Teacher, Peabody Terrace Children's Centre

~

Starting with the idyllic beauty of the Institute campus, Fellows were soon thrown into a world they would have never imagined. When Madhumita first visited the community one hot afternoon, there were long lanes with convoluted pipes. The gutter was open and contained rotting meat, thrown into it from a nearby butcher's shop.

She could see a huge hill and was told it was a mountain of garbage. Little did she know that her school was next to the place where *all* of Mumbai's garbage got dumped. On her first day, she walked into class to see one child strangling another and for weeks, parents would ask which religion she practiced. Her steadfast reply was that wasn't important; what was important, she'd tell them, was that she was teaching their children.

Amit Kumar and Vishal Kataria's school had no water in their school bathrooms. Every morning at 7 am, they'd have to pour water from buckets in the urinals so that they wouldn't clog and overflow. Venil Ali and Kanika Saraff's school had Muslim children from different sects who refused to sit next to each other. There were even some children who, in the name of religion, would flagellate themselves with whips. Anirrban Mukherjee and Meghna Mamtura's school was barricaded until 7:30 pm one night as riots had broken out in the community between Shia and Sunni Muslims over the death of a gang member. Anirrban grew a beard to better assimilate into the community. Anasuya Menon has a vivid account of the day a young woman stripped and jumped off the roof of a building. The hardship of her life had become too much for her to bear; her being naked was the only way she could be sure that no one would come near enough to stop her. Gaurav Singh's student was tied down while her parents put chilli powder in her eyes because she didn't get good marks.

Drinking was a problem in the community, and many of our 10-year-old students had been exposed to pornography because their elder siblings watched it at home. Physical abuse in the community was commonplace and accepted as a part of life. Teach For India students sometimes came to school beaten and humiliated. Parents would often tell Fellows that they should use corporal punishment with students if needed; changing a mindset that had existed for generations on how to discipline a child proved difficult.

There were also communities that welcomed Fellows and staff with the largest, most generous hearts. These were families who were grateful when Shrutika tried to break down communal tension by visiting every Eid or Ganpati. Families who were touched every time Anirrban would visit to talk about how special their child really was. Families who were surprised and delighted to see Ritesh Mishra and Charag Krishnan often spend up to six hours in the community, or when Aniket chose to live in the community alongside his students. These families affectionately called Fellows 'Didi' or 'Bhaiya' and, in any way they could, Fellows tried to be there for their families.

~

The first day of school was filled with chaotic joy: a 'Read baby, read!' chant, phonics bingo, handmade welcome crowns, and children being greeted with high-fives and warm smiles. Fellows introduced themselves not as teachers but as Didis and Bhaiyas. Tanvi baked her students' cookies, remembering how she felt when her first-grade teacher did the same for her years before. She took these cookies to her new school—a tiny set of rooms lost in the middle of a large Mumbai urban slum redevelopment project.

Another Fellow, Kanika, had an 'I Have a Dream' chart filled with little chits describing each child's aspirations.

When a small boy named Muslim's turn came, he looked a bit traumatized as he came up with a blank chit. Kanika looked at him affectionately and explained to the class how hard it is to really think about what you want to do with your life and how Muslim was thinking *so* hard that he needed one more night to think. She then looked at him (who by now was standing much straighter and even starting to smile) and said, 'Will you get it to me tomorrow, Muslim?' In that one instant, she had built his self-esteem.

Anasuya decided to read Shel Silverstein's *The Giving Tree* to her children. The story of the tree that gives and gives had been taught at the Institute and she thought her children would love it in the way that she had. Instead, her students hurled abuses at her. She remembers it poured that day, the tin roof leaking on her head. For three months, she didn't have a regular classroom and instead taught in the corridor, or any empty room. There was no blackboard; there were no benches, nowhere to put up the posters she had carefully made. Aniket remembers his first recess, when his 56 4th-grade children ran out onto the field. There was a lot of yelling and two of his boys almost killed each other. His classroom desks were falling apart because his children had stolen the iron from the bench legs to sell in the market.

Anirrban, imitating Aamir Khan in *Taare Zameen Par*, dressed like a clown on the first day of school and danced to the song 'Bum bum bole'. Only unlike Aamir, half of Anirrban's class asked him when he was going to leave and the moment the costume came off, the children went back to being disruptive. It would take months before you'd see Anirrban, still clowning around, followed by a trail of children in the community, now laughing and singing along with him.

Manu's classroom in Pune was cramped, containing 48 2nd-grade students aged 6-11. Children would fall ill every other day as the school was located next to two garbage plants, spreading a foul stench and attracting swarms of flies. There were only two toilets in the school serving 500 children. Manu taught six hours a day without a break. His kids could not speak a word of English and they couldn't write. Within the first week, his voice was gone, his energy drained, and his clothes covered with chalk powder.

Fellows often struggled to find ways to interact with the other teachers in school. In Aniket's school, his co-teacher brought her three-month old child to work every day. In Shrutika's school, a teacher would hit students in the face with his notebook. In Venil's, there was often a classroom without *any* teaching happening. Fellows would be constantly reminded that building relationships of love and trust could solve the most seemingly insurmountable problems. In one of their training sessions, Aditya Natraj, the founder of Kaivalya Education Foundation and longtime advocate for children, told them that real change in their school would start when they were invited to dinner at the most distant, difficult teacher's home.

The team was amazed by each Fellow's spirit. Manu learnt to focus on anything that was positive: a child who brought a flower to school for him or his children learning a few new words. Shrutika and her co-Fellow Vipul built classroom walls to cut out some of the deafening noise, and transformed their classrooms into beautiful spaces with inspiring paintings. Aniket got his children to do an

'I believe' art workshop, imagining the world in a different way. Surya Pratap had an amazing 'trip to Goa' investment plan where his children could earn apples and gold tickets to reach an imaginary 'Goa'. Sanket Patil was handling a class of ninety children squeezed on to benches meant for only forty; simply figuring out a system for the children to use the bathroom that didn't waste inordinate amounts of precious time was a challenge. When thirty of Sanket's students finally got transferred months later, Sanket found teaching sixty easy. Rahul Gupta's lessons were delivered with so much passion that parents of students from older grade levels were even asking to shift their kids into his class.

Shaheen walked into Subashini Rajasekharan's class one day—a class with approximately sixty students that was completely out of control. 'It was awful to watch Subashini struggle—her voice had gone and her children just wouldn't listen. I stepped in to try and help her control the class, but failed miserably. After class, instead of being dejected Subashini smiled and said to me, "Tomorrow will be better. Don't worry—we all have bad teacher days."' The next day *was* better.

~

For months after the first day, Anasuya's class continued to be violent. Each day included brutal fights, pencils stabbings and kids bleeding. Her students would bring little stones to school to fling at each other. One day, just for fun, they poured water on her iPod. They'd drink alcohol, smoke, and watch pornography. All of this was commonplace in their community. Students would witness incidents that included a three-month-old baby being flung off the high terrace of a building only because she was a girl. They'd see a woman set on fire in a dowry crime. Shocked and angry, Anasuya was determined to focus on building values. Each day, her class would work on the basics, on how to care for one another. One step at a time, they began to change.

Manu remembers the day one of his girls, after months of trying to learn Math, came to him and proudly stated that she had got her Math question right. He remembers the bus ride home that day seemed 'magical'; a child had begun to believe she could do something that she previously thought she never could.

Sanaya's classroom had an asbestos-filled ceiling that was full of holes. During the monsoon she had to strategically place her students to avoid the fifteen spots in the classroom where the water dripped. One day a child screamed as three snakes were seen wriggling into the classroom from the holes in the ceiling. Without flinching, Sanaya said they were not poisonous, and repeated aloud the class chant: '1, 2, 3, eyes on me!' Every child in the room continued to focus on the lesson, until someone from the snake park arrived to rescue the snakes.

A few weeks into teaching, Fellows soon learnt that it was essential to develop an internal locus of control; to focus solely on what was within their control.

Fellows were learning that the pressure for students to pass the state exam was extreme. They were often tempted into forcing students to memorize content, rather than ensuring meaningful learning. Fellows and staff agonized over how to solve this problem together. Their kids were several *years* behind where they needed to be. They were learning that the recruitment team wasn't kidding when they asked, 'Are you ready for a challenge?'

No one had signed up for dripping roofs, snakes, let alone disease or family tragedies. Perhaps the Yellow Hat kept all the darker things at bay, protecting the ideals that existed under each one of them. More likely, it was the relentless commitment that the staff and Fellows had towards their children's learning. Programme Managers played the role of friend, guide, teacher, parent, and coach—though often not quite adequately. Staff members experienced their own emotional ups and downs, and at times felt completely lost when supporting Fellows. They were using inadequate tools and struggled to help Fellows with many common tasks, including assessments, content, and community issues. There was a lot of energy amongst the Niners, but perhaps even more stress. Fellows would lose perspective easily and often.

Teach For India staff would bring Fellows together every Sunday after an exhausting week at school, but didn't have answers to many of the Fellows' questions. They were learning alongside their Fellows, with Shaheen perpetually reiterating a common statement, 'Keep talking to us, tell us what is and isn't working'.

Many of these struggles had an impact on culture as well, as Fellows complained of things such as unequal allocations of opportunities. When Hillary Clinton spoke to the Fellows on a trip to India, many questioned the selection process. Rumours spread quickly, and there was a need to both listen to Fellows' grievances and stress the importance of trust.

Shaheen would write to all Fellows in an email:

'And for me, if there is one thing that will kill this movement it is a lack of trust, and the hope and belief that we have in each other. No systems, or processes, or rules, or guidelines will ever be clear enough to make things seem fair and just. Each one of us has the hard work of building our culture in front of us—a culture that only the closest families have, one where members trust and love and care for each other. It is not the number of Fellows that we recruit, or the quality of them, or the results we get in our classrooms that are fundamental to us meeting our mission. It is the foundation of values we build today. If we want to grow as human beings, let's make this movement one where we care, trust, believe, and ask. This doesn't happen in most companies, in most colleges, in most families even. But who says we have to be like everyone else? I thought we were here to change the world.'

∼

Jayeshbhai was a man whose father had been a friend to Gandhiji. Having grown up since the age of nine living Gandhian values with joviality, he acted with love in every little thing that he did, setting an example that would change Shaheen's life forever. Over the years Shaheen would go to him when she was frustrated, worried about a crisis, or when she just felt exhausted. If she didn't know the outcome of something, he would share stories, such as the example of the flashlight: *One should keep focused on the ray of light, and not on the blackness beyond. When one walked the visible path of light with sincerity, the flashlight would always show you the next leg of your journey.*

Shaheen chose Ahmedabad as the place for Fellows and staff to stop, take a step back, and pause for a moment to look forward. Exhausted and overwhelmed from their first six months of teaching, Fellows and staff arrived at the Sabarmati Ashram, where Gandhiji had planned India's freedom movement. For the Fellows, days in Ahmedabad were spent connecting with the community. Fellows were paired with families and spent a day living their lives. Saahil spent his day peeling bananas to fry into banana chips, Gaurav drove a rickshaw, Shaheen sorted out garbage.

On their last day in Ahmedabad, they gathered with over 100 Fellows from Indicorps and the Gandhi Fellowship. Raising his hand to speak, Fellow Tarun Cherukuri stated that this gathering of Fellows felt like India's second fight for Independence—the fight for true social justice, liberty, equity, and fraternity. He raised a question that would stay with Teach For India for years: *'What would it take to build a young leader for India with the intellect of Nehru, the moral fibre of Gandhiji, and the compassion of Mother Teresa?'*

Something shifted inside many of them over those days and the Teach for India vision felt somehow more significant, they felt more connected to *why* they were here. This was beginning to feel like a movement.

Ahmedabad laid the seeds of what would later become formally known as Seva, a new Teach For India core value. Staff and Fellows began demonstrating small examples of Seva in unexpected ways. Fellows proudly changed their email signature to include their class name, grade, and school name. They gave away food and spread joy through music. Notes of support and gratitude became a big part of Teach For India culture. Staff members would leave colourful little notes after classroom visits; Fellows would write similar notes to their students. An all@teachforindia email address, which included all Fellows and staff, ensured the group stayed connected. They would write to each other about a range of ideas, from personal concerns and classroom ideas, to simply reaching out to communicate with one another.

Simply put, Ahmedabad accelerated the development of Teach For India's culture. After the retreat, the team created a culture document that included both principles and practices: honest and direct communication; regular informal time; celebrating positives; understanding the reality of communities; and staying closely connected with the lives of children and Fellows. Time for reflection was prioritized, with regular opportunities for people to come together outside of the office to share stories and reconnect. Each week, staff members would dedicate one morning to teach in a classroom. One of the most powerful early staff retreats occurred in a small village in Maharashtra where the team offered to cook lunch for the local residents. Cutting vegetables, cooking in a deep pit in the ground, serving others, eating together, connecting with children—these experiences kept the staff connected to their shared purpose. Festivals were celebrated, and Diwali brought a new way of thinking about light. They realized ultimately that this was a journey of light—of finding the light in each of them, in each other, and of spreading this light to the children they touched.

~

The second half of the year was a turning point for most Fellows. They were now used to their children, had management and planning practices that worked, and were seeing actual progress in their students. Now Fellows began to set more ambitious goals for themselves and their children. Surya and Saurabh began to experiment with a model to teach their children leadership. Fiona, along with a small group of Niners, travelled to visit Teach For America classrooms and came back with a new sense of possibility. Tarun and Aditya were determined that their students, who were now entering grade three, would complete a full-fledged production of the *Lion King* by the end of the year. Shaheen was amazed as she watched the performance, and would write an email the day after. Just a year earlier these children could not speak a single simple grammatically correct sentence.

> *'I spent the evening enthralled, crying happy tears and feeling the power of what we can do—the power of transformation—so deeply. And with me, another 1000-odd people watched—local government officials, school principals, parents, Fellows and most importantly, hundreds of children. I know each one of those people left carrying with them a tremendous amount of belief in human potential. One Fellow told me at the end, "They've set the bar so high". And I was thinking of how true that is, and how wonderful. Because when you see something like this, you KNOW it's possible. And when you know it's possible, you know **you** can do it, too. And with this knowledge, you can meet this bar—and maybe even set a new one.'*

After a year-long roller coaster of hard work, dreams, and emotions, Fellows spent the summer completing internships across the country that would broaden their understanding of education and enable them to think about their careers after the Fellowship. Manu went to Ladakh and spent a month in a Buddhist school, teaching a leadership module that resulted in a full-fledged student election, while he lived with one of his students in the community. Saahil and Gaurav moved to Mumbai from Pune that summer, to become part of a group of Niners who would support the Mumbai municipality in a programme it was embarking on to reform Mumbai's public schools.

> *'I met the Teach For India Fellows for the first time during my stint with the Municipal Corporation of Greater Mumbai, and was amazed to see their commitment to education. The classrooms were learning laboratories for the students as well as the Fellows. They had a distinctly joyful and lively atmosphere. The students exhibited a newfound confidence; I could see the joy of learning in the eyes of the children who were mostly coming from economically weaker family backgrounds. More surprisingly, the Fellows looked equally excited as they acquired new leadership and mentoring skills. Teach For India had provided a unique platform for the teachers and those they taught. It was a new India in the making.'*
>
> —Ashish Kumar Singh, former Additional Municipal Commissioner (Education) and Principal Secretary to the Chief Minister, Maharashtra

~

While most of the team's long waking hours were spent supporting the Fellows, children, and classrooms, there was also the work of building Teach For India. Staff also experienced significant challenges. They entered roles without clear job descriptions and definite goals, had never-ending work hours, and used outdated computers that were difficult to obtain. Running around all day and working half the night, staff often fell sick. They grappled with endless questions. What should learning look like in Teach For India classrooms? How best could support be structured? How could impact spread beyond the classroom? The answers to these led to new curricular resources and online tools to support Fellows. It also spurred initiatives like 'Be The Change Project', which required Fellows to choose and address an issue that was impeding learning in the wider school or community.

Through chaotic days staff strived to be high-energy, resourceful, and calm. Garima Kapila, Teach For India's first Mumbai City Director, described the early days.

> *'Fellows had long commutes to training sessions that would end at ten at night and would reach home at midnight. Staff made endless visits in search of schools and were appalled by the conditions in some. Fellows in the same school couldn't get along; schools would insist that Fellows fill in thick registers with student information in different coloured ink while wanting to know why they couldn't use excel spreadsheets to save time; a teacher spoke rudely to a Fellow; a parent wanted their son or daughter to leave the Fellowship to do something different.'*

Garima was always calm and rational—where there was no system, she'd develop one and put it in place. Along with Chaitali Sheth, her counterpart in Pune, she took endless steps to turn the chaos into order.

The team was small and the dream was big, and it never seemed like everything that needed to be done was actually getting done. There was the need to diversify and strengthen funding, put processes in place, leverage technology effectively, and also accurately and effectively capture impact.

Shaheen remembers being asked by a small group of Fellows to meet her at the Café Coffee Day in Pune. She was ill prepared for the seven-paged typed list of strong complaints about Teach For India, which they read out to her. They compiled a list of grievances ranging from delayed responses to salary queries to the fairness of selection criteria for events. Shaheen was always open to feedback, but by her own admission when it crossed the line into taking criticism, that had never been her strong suit. She stoically asked them for a little time to respond, and took the document home. She felt ambushed by the Fellows' collective action, hurt and deeply upset. Then she realized the deep ownership that this gesture, however hard it was to receive, indicated. *Who does that if they don't care?* With this belief, she sifted through that feedback, understood its value, and got back to them with genuine appreciation. Only all together could Teach for India be made better.

Fellows were called on for everything—to come into recruitment presentations and share their story or to speak at fund-raising evenings. In a meeting to request funding support for Teach For India, Saahil sat on the floor in one of India's most illustrious corporate leaders, Ratan Tata's, office to role-play a classroom situation and to bring to life what his world was like as a Teach For India Fellow. Charag asked his previous employer from Bharat Petroleum to visit his class, and then spoke to him each week, which lead to a real belief and significant corporate donation to Teach For India. Rakesh Mani suggested a design for a tool to measure the performance of Fellows; Madhumita wrote online articles encouraging new Fellows to join. Fellows would do anything to make their kids happy, incessantly watching a demoralized Indian cricket team play a losing match because of their 'Sense of Possibility', and would sometimes literally cry like babies when they saw a once-struggling and blocked child now reading 50 words per minute.

~

'The most powerful elixirs were the little moments of the classroom. When my class "pick-pocket" became the proud keeper of the lost-and-found corner, when Sunam conquered decoding and his grades catapulted across the board, when Vamshi asked about the universe with stars almost twinkling in his eyes, when the lesson plan worked beyond how I'd imagined it. Overall, the classroom was the toughest but also the most rewarding part of the Fellowship experience.'

— Sana Gabula, 2009 Teach For India Alumnus, MBA from the Graduate Student, Columbia Business School and currently exploring Technology in Education

At the end of the two years, twelve of Manu's students scored a 95 percent on the nationwide, competitive ASSET test in Math. All of his children, who were not able to write words two years earlier, published a book in English with their own thoughts proudly expressed. On the last day of school he gifted each of his children these books. His children hadn't just learnt writing; they had learnt freedom of expression. Manu learnt that he could play a role in helping his children find their own destiny. He could help to make them count.

Fiona Vaz and Vaibhav Mathur set the ambitious goal for their students to read 200 books by the end of the Fellowship. Fuelled by her visit to a Teach For All conference in the US, where she witnessed a high-performing charter school with students each reading 200 books a year, Fiona came back at the end of her first year of teaching convinced her students could accomplish something similar. Vaibhav and Fiona hosted a book drive and collected thousands of books. Their kids had 199 days of school; they needed to read a book a day. In just 70 days Madhu had read 260 books. By the end of the year, the class average was 173 books. This was what was possible.

Tarun and Aditya's students went from not speaking a word of English in grade 2 to performing a 90-minute production of the *Lion King* at the end of grade 3. The performance was astounding. Tarun and Aditya had found people to replicate the Broadway costumes, raised funding to rent a community space, and mobilized families to bring more than 800 people to the performance. Perhaps most stunning was the process that the children went through over the year to reach that final performance. Like Simba in the *Lion King*, their students too examined many of the values embedded in the play—fear, confidence, the circle of life, and human interdependence. In that year, using Teach For India's starting assessments that would grow in rigor over the following years, they made 2.5 years of academic growth.

The happiest day in Vipul Shaha's two years in the Fellowship came when a girl in his class was offered a place at the residential Sahyadri School run by the Krishnamurthi Foundation near Pune. In his previous conversations with her mother, he became aware of the harsh realities of this girl's life, the punishments she suffered, and the unrealistic expectations her family placed on her. Her family planned to move back to their village in Rajasthan and get this extremely bright and sensitive girl married while she was still underage. Determined to keep her in school, he spent a year in conversations, follow-up visits, and entrance tests, and managed to get the Sahyadri School, without any existing precedent, to offer her a sponsored seat. More than anything, this experience taught him the power of belief in another human being, and what it truly meant to live for a higher purpose.

Each one of the Niners learnt from their experiences, often times in extremely painful ways.

Milind lost his second-grade student Pawan. A day earlier, Pawan was playing in a garden near his home and ate a plant, mistaking it for sugarcane. He developed a violent reaction and was dead hours later. Pawan's mother was on dialysis, his father had passed away, and only an ageing grandfather was there to look after him. Pawan was slow to learn, but he was the hope for the whole family. He enjoyed school and started bringing stories of class home to his mother. Milind realized that no one would take responsibility for Pawan—the police said they couldn't do anything, the plant in the garden had since disappeared, the doctor didn't have the time to see him. Sitting in Pawan's home the next day, acutely aware of the emptiness, Milind felt hollow. He realized that every moment mattered in bringing unconditional love, connection, mentorship, and meaning into the life of his children, and made a promise to himself that he would always serve.

Anasuya struggled with her school Principal to get time and space to teach and would often come home in tears. One day, realizing she didn't have the same faith in her school Principal that she strived to have in her students, she wrote her Principal a ten-page letter. The letter described why she joined Teach For India and what she wanted for their children. She was surprised at the acknowledgement that came through in the principal's response. This small act taught Anasuya humility and the importance of faith. She learnt never to lower the bar for kids, however much they are struggling at home. With that learning, her students made 1.5 years of growth in their second year. They were starting, slowly, to bridge the gap. Anasuya would say of her Fellowship, 'I have lived a lifetime in these two years. I have journeyed from Anasuya to Ana Didi, from student to teacher, from planner to executor, from musing over problems to finding their solutions, from being judgemental and opinionated to giving faith a chance and truly believing in the potential of people. I could go on and on.'

Indira Aditi took her students on a field trip to a top Mumbai College. She overheard her children in conversation, telling each other how much they liked the college and asking each other how they could get there.

Little Anurag told the others, 'only those who clear our big goal in Math and English will get there.' 'Yes,' replied Hemant, 'we will all go there together.'

Abhik's children were four years behind their private school peers when he left Britannia Industries to teach them. He was challenged to be patient and nurturing to his fifty children every single day. He learnt to practice control, understanding, and humility even when he saw corporal punishment take place in front of him in the school. He learnt to be resourceful when the school needed a library, or when he wanted his children to go on a field trip. He learnt that change truly began by re-engineering his internal dialogue, his prejudices, and his limiting mindset. He learnt to see beauty in the most unlikely places.

'An unhealthy rose, pressed between soiled newspapers in a handmade envelope and presented to me on my first day in the classroom. A brown and black-checkered handkerchief made out of organza and polyester, in 10-year-old Akash's fist as he wiped the tear that was stealing the twinkle from his eye. A Math worksheet, without a single cross, after eight months of not giving up as 6-year-old Faizal beams and says, "Chalo, teach me more." Waiting at the hospital as 5-year-old Zaheer's head is bandaged, blood drops and teardrops smudging his face as the relentless smile persisted. A trip to the airport, where 11-year-old Jugal says, "Hurry up and teach me English. All the flight manuals are in English." An old black Bata shoe, painted in magenta and submerged in gold and silver glitter, as 11-year-old Amir tells me, "With this shoe on, I can go away, to my dreams. But,

Sir, you won't fit into this shoe.'"

—Abhik Bhatacharjee, 2009 Teach For India Alumnus, Teacher Coach at Teach For Slovakia, Strategic Marketing, Dasra

Romana Sheikh and Ivan Dias wanted to see change across their school. As slightly unsure but very driven second-year teachers, they started doing optional language training sessions for other teachers in their school. They were amazed at the results; word walls were now up on walls of other Teach For India classrooms, discussions in the staff room revolved around how to teach through activities and games, countdowns for classroom management replaced more traditional disciplining techniques, teachers spoke to children in English and children replied in English, and you could see distinctly more collaboration amongst teachers.

At the end of the two years, the Niners were back on a stage, this time to mark the end of the Fellowship. Shaheen opened a storybook and read a story of the Fellowship's journey through the eye of a Firki, while Somika Basu, then Teach For India's Communication Director, *became* the Firki onstage. Gaurav's graduation speech evoked awe. By memorizing 87 sentences, describing every one of the Niners in alphabetical order, he brought to life how well he knew each one. The staff team who had supported the Niners made a video of all the hopes they held for them. Ruchi Jain wanted them to embrace the unknown. Kovid Gupta wanted them to live life big, like a Bollywood film. Sheela Prasad wanted them to choose the path that scared them the most. Gayatri Lobo wanted them to remember that together, they could do this. Shaheen, she wanted them to dream and to find their greatest colours.

places you

CHAPTER 8

THIS IS REAL

'I remember taking my place on the balcony of YB Chavan Hall in Mumbai, alongside friends and colleagues from the 2010 cohort, all of us excited to watch the 2009 Fellows graduate and take their first steps as Alumni. I remember the sense of immense pride as I watched the members of the cohort make their way on to the stage one last time. And then it happened: in one spontaneous moment, all of us on the balcony stood up to give the Niners a standing ovation. But in that split second, the Niners too all looked up and our gaze met theirs. It was a simple and fleeting exchange but one that we would not forget, for the mantle of leadership and responsibility had been passed on to us. It felt powerful. It felt real. It felt like a movement had begun.'

—Arhan Bezbora, 2010 Teach For India Alumnus and Senior Manager, Alumni Impact, Teach For India

137 Fellows joined the movement in May 2010, and 260 Fellows would join a year later. Building on what the Niners had done, they were able to be better, faster. They were called the Tenners. In this year, 3853 applicants had competed for 150 seats, and selectivity was at 6.8 percent. It was important to keep the bar on selection incredibly high; the people Teach For India was searching for were India's future leaders.

2010 was an important milestone for Teach For India. The Niners had aligned with an idea, but the Tenners had joined a movement that existed. The Tenners made Teach For India *real*. No longer was it a one-year experiment, they were now part of a movement that would last. The 2011 cohort, called the Eleveners, was hugely exciting; it was four times the size of the first cohort and double the size of the Tenners. Every additional Fellow meant more lives changed in the short-term, and one more leader fighting for equity in education in the long-term. Imagining each cohort before they arrived at Institute was incredibly exciting, the night before was always hard to sleep.

~

The next two years were filled with more and more stories,

and a greater sense of possibility. Proof of academic excellence was now visible in some Teach For India classrooms, and this was a critical lever in fuelling the belief that what had once appeared overwhelmingly impossible could actually come to be.

There were always these little miracles of effort and belief that kept everyone inspired. Srini Srinivasan's classroom echoed with creativity. His second standard 'responsible champions' came to class to find a cotton-candy vendor in class to teach them sequencing through making their own pink fluff, or were in awe of the real live tortoise that had travelled in the local train with Srini to enact the 'Hare and the Tortoise' story. Srini wanted to give his children the world. He showered them with love and piqued their imagination. He would dress up as a word chef so his children could stick words on to his apron, and made a makeshift screen of a clean white sheet to show his students an Apple app that took them inside the human body.

Rohita Kilachand's student Shah Jahan would always find new ways of disrupting class, since studying was always the last thing on his mind. One day Rohita discovered that Shah Jahan's grandmother would tie his hands to a bed every afternoon, and then leave. At first angry, Rohita then tried to understand.

> *'I learnt that no one person was at fault. If I really wanted to create a long-term difference to the child and in turn, his education, I had to start asking "Why" and delving deeper. I came to know that his grandmother and mother worked at an agarbatti factory every day, for long hours, to make their living. Since they did not have any relatives*

to take care of Shah Jahan while they were away, they believed it was best to tie him to the bed for "safety". This was bizarre for me to even accept, but actually, both mother and grandmother were very nice people. And both had miserable stories to tell—of abuse from either their husbands or from people at work. They did what they thought best for Shah Jahan. This is not to justify what he went through, simply to understand it.'

—Rohita Kilachand, 2010 Teach For India Alumnus and Founder, The Warehouse

Rohita learnt the value of collective understanding and belief from her Programme Manager. She would say,

'If my mentor never gives up on me, I will never give up on my child! How simple, and how powerful is that lesson? When my mentor shows me that I am capable of a certain standard of teaching and responsibility, no matter what is going on in my life, I will in turn, lovingly, expect nothing less from my child.'

Archana Rao independently raised enough money so that her children could fly to Indian School of Business (ISB) in Hyderabad. She wanted them to know that they could be in a great college like ISB one day if they worked hard enough.

Sachin Paranjpe's class was down a grim hall that reeked of the school bathroom, but one would enter the door of his classroom and be in a different world. Incense burned, every class would end with a values session where children would bravely and openly talk about what they didn't like about how they were that day.

During his first year, Arhan shared a reflection on a balloon with his cohort.

> *'We are all so different, and yet we're going in one direction. That means it's not enough to be strong individuals with different opinions and answers, but that we must become a group of strong individuals committed to finding the best answer for our mission. Like the balloon, how light we are determines how fast the balloon moves up. And it is with humility and the ability to laugh at ourselves and not take ourselves too seriously that we will move up.'*

He remembers his Programme Manager being asked by a confused Principal why Fellows came dressed up as bumble bees. Arhan's class had been in the middle of the chapter on bees in their textbook, and Arhan believing in bringing learning to life, turned into a bumble bee for his students.

Shashank Shukla spent the summer after his first year in Delhi talking to homeless people all night for a month. At the end of the summer, he was determined to find a way to work with children who had even greater needs than those he had taught in his first year as a Fellow in the low-income private school in Pune. He transferred to Ummeed, a residential school for street and juvenile children aimed at integrating street children back into society through a combination of love, protection, and skill building.

> *'In my first week at Ummeed, I talked to my children about the virtues of following rules and obeying teachers.*

Malik looked at me angrily and said, "Have you ever wondered what it feels like to sleep on the floor instead of your comfortable bed? Have you ever wondered how it feels to be seen as a criminal all the time even if you are innocent? What would that make you?" Before I could answer, he answered the question himself. "A criminal," he said, loudly and defiantly.

'All of my children had similar stories; they had run away due to abuse, addictions, or abject poverty. On the streets, they got into theft, beggary, hooliganism, and drug peddling. My children had learnt to survive the world with pride as their weapon, defiance as their nature, and mistrust as their motto. Now in front of them they had a teacher armed with charts and markers. I told them that the cost of defiance would be severe—a black star on their copies or half an hour of extra studies. They were first amused, then defiant, and finally dismissive of my classroom strategies and average attendance was less than 40 percent. I knew that I was failing as a teacher.

'One morning, I saw my student Ajay fighting with a boy from a nearby school who had called him, "anaath" or an orphan. I gathered the class, telling them that the most important thing was what they thought of themselves. If they believed in themselves, they would not waste themselves in drugs, violence and hate and hide behind a false sense of pride I told them they had two choices—to fight those who insulted them, or to do something that would force the world to give them respect.

'We drew up an improbable goal: secure admissions on their own merit in class 9 in a reputed English medium school. In one year, they'd need to learn what other *children needed to learn in 4.5 years in order to be at the same level. I started spending nights at Ummeed as the exams drew near, and on the day of the exam, I sat outside praying. The results came; all 27 of my children secured admission into class 9.*

'In my second year, another Fellow, Saloni Gupta, took over my class. She had apprehensions; could a 26-year-old woman with a background in software engineering do this? We failed often, but our children continued to get up at 4 am, study from 8 am to 11 pm, taking breaks only for lunch and volleyball. Every student passed his or her 9th standard exams. After this, Saloni and I left Ummeed, overcome by the guilt of leaving our students when they most needed us and although we kept in touch with our children frequently, we feared the worst. And then, the day the 10th standard CBSE Board results came out, I got a message from Saloni. "Congratulations, Shashank Bhaiya,' it said, "All of our students have graduated."'

—Shashank Shukla, 2010 Teach For India Alumnus; Mason Fellow, Harvard Kennedy School; Chairman, Gurukul Group of Institutions.

~

Fellows thought about impact beyond the classroom too. Sachin, Vikas, and Arhan started a programme called 'Just For Kicks' as a way to introduce football to their 3rd standard students. Little Chaitrali was the team manager, and students were the football coaches who then coached other students. Just For Kicks grew to cover over 54 schools across Mumbai and Pune. Its motto was powerful: *Everyone* Plays. Ashwin Bhatnagar and Sunny Guptan were passionate about ending corruption; they organized in schools across Pune an anti-corruption campaign called 'What Will I Do About It?' where students drew a vision of change for a corrupt-free India. Anurag Malloo travelled to the Antarctic, and planted a Teach For India flag firmly in the ice there. And Anirrban tattooed a Firki on his arm that would serve as a constant reminder of his commitment to the movement.

Proof points of excellence, both in Teach For India and across the network, began to demonstrate what was possible. High expectations of what their children could achieve served as a powerful example to set ambitious goals in one's own classroom. Sanaya Bharucha named her class the Explorer Class, and taught through values and songs. Starting at below a kindergarten level, her children were soon multiplying two digit numbers and speaking English in full paragraphs. They learnt with joy and fun; writing poems, learning drama and elocution, and singing songs that Sanaya found or made up for many topics. Students were able to articulate how English would help increase their job opportunities in the city of Pune and about how not doing your homework was just going to make you less intelligent.

Sana Gabula came to class and found six shiny magnets missing. Before reacting, she thought, *Why not give belief a chance?* With her brightest smile, she turned to the 35 young faces and asked all of them to look for the magnets and return them to the board so that the whole class could use them. There was no finger pointing or bag-checking. Sana just kept repeating, 'I believe in you, in us, and that we are a great class that works together.' That day, 4 of the 6 magnets were returned and the next day, so were the remaining 2. Sana learnt that she could see the world in a different way through the lens of belief.

As Fellows demonstrated the little steps that defined an excellent education, they pushed Teach For India staff to evolve its student vision. This wasn't just about math and language; it wasn't just about measuring years of academic growth. This was about values and mindsets, exposure, and access. Sanaya's students had made almost three years of academic growth in a year, but they were only able to achieve this through her strong focus on their values and mindsets. Archana's trip to ISB exposed her children to the idea of having an ambitious goal, and set in place a compelling *why* for her kids to work towards. Tarun and Aditya's *Lion King* had been a powerful example of all three; exposure to the arts, deepening their commitment to life values, and seeing all this translate into dramatic academic gains.

'Teach For' organizations from across the world shared proof points of excellent classrooms. Teach For America's Sue Lehman Award recognized some of Teach For America's most transformational teachers, and classroom videos of teachers served as inspiring examples. Teach For India staff and Fellows had opportunities to travel abroad to learn directly from the global network. In the first Teach For All trip to New York in 2010, Fellows were shaken by the question 'What will your kids be like without you?' They came back with a fundamentally different bar of excellence to aspire to, in their classrooms.

~

India was host to the first large Teach For All Global Conference where staff and teachers from 14 countries around the world came to Mumbai to focus on 'The Change Within'. Teach For All wanted to learn from Teach For India's first steps in personal transformation, community immersion, and building culture. Shaheen wrote to her team just before the conference:

> *'I need you all to do what you always do when our friends are here. I need you to share, openly, your successes and challenges. I need you to tell your amazing stories of change and hope. I need you to shower our guests with hospitality and care and love. I need you to infuse your sense of possibility into every interaction that you have. I need you to make each conversation deep, and meaningful. I hope you give freely of your thoughts and your experiences. And I hope you take away inspiration.'*

The conference enabled participants from across the globe to connect with children and listen to them, to immerse themselves in local communities and observe themselves in the process, to engage in rich dialogue with each other about what it would take to get to the collective vision. Participants left with a deeper understanding of the need for reflection, of involving communities more in Teach For India's work, of sharing stories, of thinking of values, and academics. They left with Gandhiji's thought that 'my life is my message'; that in the end this is deeply personal work. They left feeling inspired by what India, with its scale and complexity, aimed to achieve. Consequently, they left thinking that their countries could accomplish something similar. This was a global fight, and they had each other for support.

Teach For America participants would send thoughts from their time in India.

'I commit to daily quiet time to reflect on who I am, and what it means to be me. It is so easy to get caught up in everything around myself, and I sometimes forget to love myself enough. Therefore, I am going to spend time each day "finding myself". This is the first and most important step in me "becoming the change" I want in others around me.'

'On the plane, I vowed that I would really, truly love my students. I don't like my kids all the time, that's for sure. But underneath even the most rotten and seemingly evil child is someone shaped by unfair and uncertain circumstance, and I love that soul. I love that soul and I will do what I can to try and influence it positively. Still, sometimes I forget that it's not them I'm mad at, but the system.'

TeachFirst, in the UK, brought twenty-five members of its senior leadership team to India, including their Chairperson Dame Julia Cleverdon, to learn, reflect, and bond as a leadership team. They spent time in communities, taught in a Teach For India classroom, and participated in 'Inequity Day' where they were randomly assigned an income level and needed to live within that level for a day. Those living below the poverty line could use one bucket of cold water, slept on the floor, and had a simple, rationed vegetarian meal. It could never feel anything like real poverty, but it was a small experiment with which to practise empathy and understanding.

'The results were better than we could possibly have hoped. It required a major commitment from all of us to take a week off, and to move far outside all of our comfort zones, but I can honestly say that no week over the past nine years has been more important to the evolution of our programme and the impact we are trying to facilitate among tens of thousands of young British people.'

– Brett Wigtordz, CEO, TeachFirst

As Fellows began to see proof points of excellence in the Fellows from earlier cohorts, Teach For India's challenges evolved too. From launching Teach For India with 6 staff members, the Teach For India staff team grew to 70 by 2011. Sixteen graduating Fellows joined staff positions, enabling the team to now have their first-hand experience of the Fellowship as they made decisions as staff members. Despite opposition to the idea, Shaheen brought the young and relatively inexperienced Tomos Davies in as Teach For India's Chief Operating Officer. The difficult decision of possibly losing significant funding to hire someone she believed in paid off; Tomos was to be the fair, direct, deeply thoughtful partner that Shaheen needed to grow Teach For India.

Teach For India's budget grew from five to eleven crores. They implemented systems and processes across departments. Technology was strengthened, and Salesforce, a global cloud computing company, changed efficiency across the organization. Goals were set more strategically, and there was a definite shift from just trying to get things off the ground to thinking more clearly and planning ahead of time, therefore improving the quality of Teach for India.

Teach For India's core values continued to be at the centre of everything. New key messages were introduced to ensure a clearer, more aligned culture. These included, 'Share, share, share', 'Ask, ask, ask', 'Relationships and results', 'Be nice, be gentle', and the question, 'What will I do about it?' The 'open forum' became an important structure for people to speak and be heard. Challenges continued; the lack of hierarchy often led to everyone wanting to be involved in everything. Fellows challenged Teach For India's communication guidelines, arguing that to deny them the right to say exactly what they wanted in any forum they chose was a violation of the freedom of expression guaranteed by the Indian constitution. Fellows sometimes challenged existing methodologies related to their classrooms and this led to difficult conversations with Programme Managers on how much freedom should be allowed in the classroom.

Teach For India continued to be on a steep learning curve; many early staff members were foreigners to India from the Teach For America or Teach First programmes, and language and context was difficult for them. Rebecca showed up for her first day of work in a white suit only to realize that that may not be the most appropriate form of clothing to wear. Kate's apartment roof fell down one day when she was out running, but she kept going to work anyway. She struggled to understand how the importance of family in India could sometimes mean an absence from school for what seemed a small family commitment, and often with little notice. Alika spent countless hours just locating schools in Pune that were 'near the chicken shop past the banana stand'.

Programme Managers felt stretched and often unsuccessful. They were often managing Fellows older and more experienced than them, and the challenge of differentiating support for seventeen Fellows was hard for first-time managers. These Managers were up late at night, worked through weekends, and were often left feeling overwhelmed. Mumbai City Director Garima got malaria; Pune City Director Chaitali was playing a double role supporting twenty Fellows and running the city. Placement school issues were many; classes that were supposed to have forty students were much larger, and classes that were supposed to be larger had fewer kids. Fellows who had commited to joining the Fellowship didn't join, which led to a teacher shortage. Teach For India was doing too many things at the same time: running the Fellowship, launching a new recruitment campaign to bring in 300 new Fellows, growing the number of staff to support this number, fund-raising, planning for Teach For India's next city, and developing relationships with organizations that could potentially hire our graduating Fellows.

Perhaps the most challenging situation that Programme Managers faced were issues of child protection. Teach For India students were exposed to abuse and trauma at home and in school, and Teach For India put in place a Child Protection policy and trained Fellows on the rights of children. Many Fellows had grown up exposed to corporal punishment, and needed to understand a different way of working with children.

'What do you do when Fellows come to you and say a Principal is touching girls, or another teacher in the school is beating my students, or my child is getting sexually abused at home? What do you tell them when their student comes to school burnt or cut?'

—Aniket Thukral, 2009 Teach For India Alumnus
and Manager, Child Rights

In times that got chaotic, Shaheen would remind the first cohort of the examples they were:

'My 09 Fellows—all of us are depending on you. To lead by example, to stay positive, to spread Teach For India's culture of open communication and the values we believe in. You are the greatest support right now—to our Tenners and to us on staff. Remember we've brought in new Fellows, we are reaching thousands of more children, and we are working to double the number of schools. This has to be worth what we are all going through together right now. And I believe we can get through this calmly, with a sense of humor and fun, if we care deeply for each other, trust each other and above all, believe in each other.'

~

Time at the Institute was perhaps the most intensely charged five weeks of the year.

'The Institute is so much more than training teachers. The Institute is energy. It's love. It's movement-building. It's planting seeds. It's where magic happens. Where mindsets are built. Where values are taught. It's leadership. It's reflection. It's failure. It's resilience. Through training teachers, we learn about ourselves, our colleagues, our communities, our kids, and this movement to provide every child in the world a chance to fulfill his or her potential.'

—Maureen Ferry, former Teach For India staff member and Teacher Leadership Development Fellowship Leader, Teach For America

The five weeks were a blend of closely supervised classroom teaching, sessions on pedagogy, and on content. Institute was an introduction to the reality we were trying to change, the intensity of the Fellowship, and the culture of Teach For India. Fellows questioned more of what we did, and on the Yellow Hat day this year, Fellows questioned whether it was possible to have impact in a simulated activity over a few hours. Ajita Raghavendra was in a group that was asked to go out and feed a group of people without money or food, and when his group decided to interpret 'feed' as 'feed knowledge', he thought that was too simple and moved away from the group. Ajita spent time in the community, and decided to try to get employment for people who could then earn the money to eat for themselves. He found a homeless alcoholic man, struck up a conversation, and asked if he wanted a job. Along with his new friend Ajita went to roadside restaurants, asking if they needed to employ an extra pair of hands. Finally, one small place agreed. Ajita returned and told the story; the expression on the man's face was not something he would forget. It was possible to have impact in every moment if one truly believed.

∼

From the beginning, Teach For India understood the importance of both a strong design and communication component of the organization. Fellows and staff were encouraged to use social media to share stories and experiences, a website started to develop, and significant thought was given to how to build a brand that would define Teach For India and encourage people across India to join the movement. Recruitment campaigns focused on our mission to eliminate inequity in education, but had a strong second message built around the tremendous leadership skills Fellows would get back from the programme. Recruitment became more strategic; colleges and companies were selected to visit and the high-energy recruitment team would make thousands of presentations, followed with one on one phone calls to answer the many questions and concerns people had as they contemplated the Fellowship. Fellows interested in joining Teach For India had many hurdles to overcome, the largest being post-Teach For India career options and parental opposition. While a minority of parents were supportive of their children joining the Fellowship, many were unhappy and did not understand why their child would graduate from a top college to teach in a school for low-income children. There were several difficult conversations that staff had with parents; in one extreme case a father threatened to kill himself and have his body lain across his daughter's classroom if she joined the Fellowship.

The Communications team conceptualized creative events to get internal and external stakeholders to truly feel the spirit of Teach For India. 'Teach For India Week' was an annual week where leaders across sectors were invited to come into a classroom and teach alongside a Fellow. Leaders spanning banking and IT, HR and Consulting, Film and Media—all came in to teach. They went in nervous, led sessions based on the lesson plans given, shared life stories and experienced what it must feel like to be a teacher in a Teach For India classroom.

In 2010, Teach For India hosted the first of many inspirED conferences, conceptualized to inspire a wide range of stakeholders to do more towards the vision that one day, all children across India would attain an excellent education. Years earlier, Shaheen had attended a conference in Florida where 8000 educators had gathered to learn and share more about what it meant to be a great educator. She sat in the opening plenary amongst the 8000 hoping that one day in India, thousands of people would come together to ask the most difficult questions, and support each other to drive the most unimaginable change. InspirED was a response to that; it was a belief that Teach For India could attempt to inspire change way beyond the Fellowship.

The inspirED conferences created spaces of possibility where over 500 educators and other stakeholders came together and could choose from over 50 sessions to attend. Sessions were practical, fun, and kept children as the central focus. One could attend a session to better understand the Right to Education, or learn how to use art in the classroom, or understand data-driven instruction. Sessions were high-energy and interactive and challenged people to do more for all kids. Teach For India also hosted a TEDx around the theme of transformation in education, where 700 people came to see students, educators, actors, and business people talk about their connection to education. Akanksha student Jyoti Reddy talked about her journey from the slums, where she lost her father at the age of ten, to St. Xavier's College, and the role that her teacher Anjali had played. Jo Chopra shared how her life's work started when she adopted little Moi Moi and found out she was severely disabled. Her love for her daughter led to the creation of the Latika Roy foundation, a sensitive and beautiful school and vocational centre where every single child was loved and valued.

~

As the budget grew, so did Teach For India's need to think creatively about fundraising. Teach For India fundraisers would invite donors to fund individual classrooms and schools after hearing classroom stories. At one fundraiser, over four crores were raised, with donors excitedly bidding on schools. The small development team leveraged Fellow and staff networks to raise money. For three years in a row, Teach For India would participate in and win the India Giving Challenge, where Give India matched a part of the money raised. In the first year of the challenge alone, Fellows raised 61 lakhs through 1868 unique donors, aided by Teach For India's one lakh Facebook friends, who helped spread an awareness of its work. While funding in the first three years came largely from large foundations and corporates, the development team recognized the potential of high volume small denomination funding.

True to the original blueprint developed at McKinsey, the Teach For India team was committed to quality *and* scale. The need to expand early was driven by the belief that India not only needed great leaders, but also *enough* leaders. Delhi, the Nation's Capital was chosen for its proximity to government and policy-level change.

In 2011, Delhi launched under the grace and positivity of Sheela Prasad's leadership. Although Sheela had been with Teach For India since 2008, setting up Delhi was difficult. Teach For India did not have the network of Akanksha to rely on, and everything needed to be sourced from scratch. The tiny start-up Delhi team took the brand new Delhi metro across the vast city, walked through little gullies to find schools, started building relationships with the Delhi Municipal Corporation, and set up a small Delhi office. Sheela would write to Fellows the day before they'd first step into Delhi classrooms for the first time:

'Tomorrow you will first meet the children whose lives we are here to change. Tomorrow you will start to build confidence, joy, and care in your children, and unlock their potential. Tomorrow you will wow the Principals that will be our partners for years to come. Tomorrow you start the movement to end educational inequity in Delhi.

'I know I will remember tomorrow forever, and that you will too.'

—Sheela Prasad, Former Delhi City Director and Cluster Head, Teach For America

Delhi Fellows entered challenging environments where children were way behind where they needed to be. They had to figure out a new curriculum: what to teach, how to teach, how to track, how to ask for help, and how to figure out things on your own when there was no help to be had. Delhi started in a flurry of emotions, a sea of both unfamiliar and the warmest colours, an unpaved road with cracks and holes and breakers, all navigated with the practice of Teach For India values and monumental amount of sheer belief.

Mohit Arora and Gaurav Singh taught in a school in a community in South Delhi that even the rickshaw drivers were hesitant to visit. The school had 500 girls who ran haywire all day, and no instruction was happening. A group of male teachers sat outside chatting all day. There was no Principal, and no one wanted the job of leading the school. The children did not sing the National Anthem together during assembly, and nobody cared to lead or correct them. There was no water or electricity and heaps of garbage lay around uncollected and rotting in the sun. A teacher walked around with the face of his palm opened, ready to swat any little girl that might stumble into his way. Mohit and Gaurav swept their classroom so their little girls could sit down on the floor. On one of the run-down walls, they had written 'Be nice, be gentle'. Theirs were the only classes that ran in the school; theirs were the only girls who had a chance; the only girls who stood confidently to greet you. It was difficult to see girls from the other classes crowded at the door of Mohit and Gaurav's classroom, trying to be a part of the learning.

Nirali Vasisht and Avantika Singh taught next door to each other in a Delhi private school, and when you walked into their classrooms you saw magic. Both groups of second grade students spoke only a few words of English at the start; 18 months later they were reading and analyzing Harry Potter and the unabridged version of *Oliver Twist*, a 6th grade text. Avantika had spent the decade prior to joining the Fellowship as a news anchor on *Headlines Today*. Her dream for her kids was to get them to visit a newsroom, but only after she thought that they could think critically, speak eloquently, and had unleashed their imagination and changed their aspirations. Her students met the high bar she had set for them; on the day her kids visited, there was much joy in the newsroom where Avantika once worked before she had become a teacher, and in her heart, and in the proud hearts of her children.

A year after Teach For India launched in Delhi, Sheela would say, '*At the end of that first year, I cried tears of joy at work for the second time in my life. Our team visited a few classrooms to gain common qualitative data to assess our progress in the year. Our second grade students, who were shy at the beginning of the year, described to me in understandable but ungrammatical English, which problems in their community and world they wanted to solve. I walked out of the school and sobbed silently for reasons I didn't know at the time. I recognize now that my belief was growing.*'

~

With the graduation of the Niners, Teach For India's first cohort of Alumni began fulfilling their roles in the movement, a moment they originally envisioned two years earlier. Over 65 percent of them chose to stay in the development sector full-time, and almost all of the Alumni left committed to contributing to children from wherever they were. This was a marked increase from the 5 percent that originally knew they would wanted to be in the education sector beyond their Fellowship.

Teach For India's first Alumni took brave steps. Ashish Srivastav left for Dantewada to set up a Fellowship similar to Teach For India in the most remote tribal area. Gaurav Singh left the Fellowship with a vision of building 100 excellent schools for low-income students, and set off to the KIPP School Leader Fellowship to learn how to be an excellent school leader. Prakhar Mishra started Youth Alliance in Delhi, a way for youth to engage in social change. Sana Gabula joined McKinsey's education practice. And having never been there before, Saahil Sood moved to Hyderabad to set up Teach For India's next site.

Never had the power of an Alumni movement become as visible to Shaheen as at Teach For America's 20th year summit. 11,000 Teach For America Alumni were present. The room was filled with eminent leaders like the US Secretary of Education Arne Duncan, civil rights leader Gloria Steinem, author Malcolm Gladwell, and Harlem Children's Zone founder Geoffrey Canada. Obama's special video message said that one of the biggest impacts on a child's success comes 'from the man or woman in front of the classroom and anyone who chooses that path deserves our respect and our support'. Board member John Legend sang the song 'If You're Out There' and 'Shine' accompanied by students from the Teach For America Alumni-led organization KIPP. Sitting there, one of 11,000, listening to Legend's hauntingly beautiful voice, hearing one after the other Alumni answer the question '*What role will I play?*' with heart and conviction, Shaheen could feel the power of Wendy's original vision. It was time to build an unstoppable movement in India.

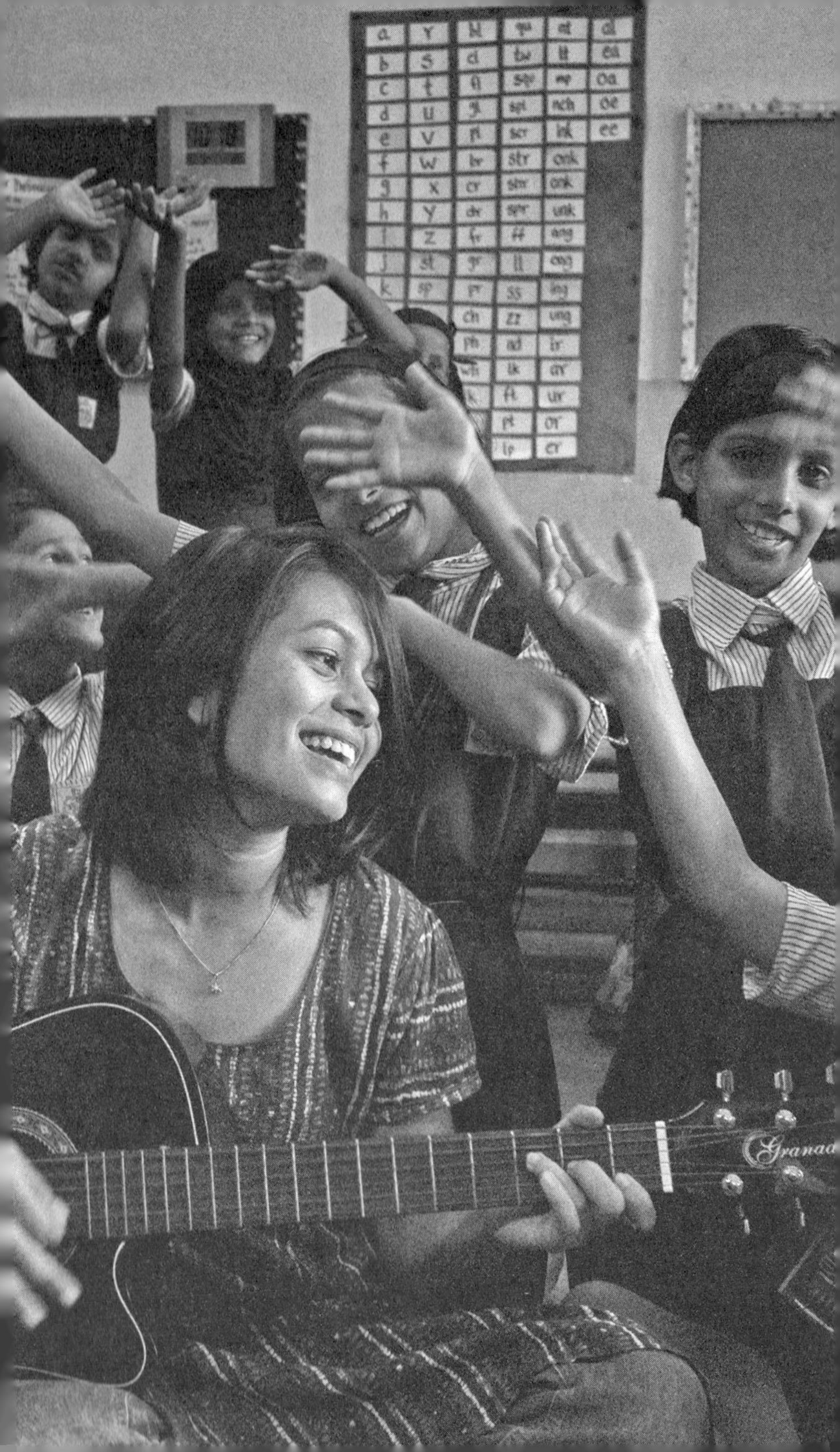

CHAPTER 9

THE COLOURS OF A MOVEMENT

'I used to think that my life was not easy; that I had seen it all. Then, after my first year of teaching, I did an internship in a small school in rural Sikkim. I was wrong; I had not seen it all. With a wooden school building and a makeshift hostel not strong enough to stand against the bone-biting cold, there have been days when the freezing wind blew viciously through the wide gaps between the wooden planks making it impossible for us to sleep. But how do you look after your students at night with no shelter when it's raining ceaselessly for 24 hours?

'When I thought it couldn't get any worse, the kids started getting sick. With no doctor around, and instances of as many as twenty children violently ill at the same time, I had no other option but to call my friends at Teach For India for solace and cry in fear and frustration over the phone behind closed doors. Here I would find the courage to put on a brave face and emerge able to maintain a real feeling of possibility for the kids and for myself. We cut and carried wood from the forests over the

roughest terrain, and took children with all their clothes to wash them in the streams far below and then have to make the steep climb back up because there had been no water supply for days.

'There were also tears of joy. I have learnt to smile in extreme conditions and to find happiness in small things. On numerous occasions when I have locked myself inside a room, pumped my fist in extreme satisfaction, and shouted with sheer exuberance like a child. These were moments when I saw school graduates getting over 70 percent in their CBSE board exams, or when the students who we worked with day in and out through their winter vacations, got admission in Delhi University. The moments when students read Roald Dahl on dark nights under candlelight, or when they played the National Anthem flawlessly on the piano, moments when they scored spectacular goals in football matches wearing mismatched pairs of torn slippers.'

—Arnab Thockder, 2012 Teach For India Alumnus and Teacher, Sikkim Himalayan Academy

Achieving educational equity for every child in India would not occur through the Fellowship alone, but rather as a result of the exponentially larger impact of the Alumni movement. This was not just about creating better teachers; this was about people committed to a lifetime of work towards achieving a dream.

Two years after the first Teach For India class of Fellows had graduated, Alumni each chose a different part of the puzzle to focus on. Chaitra Murlidhar chose the teacher training piece and joined the Thermax Social Initiatives Foundation to train teachers across Pune's municipal schools. Mayank Lodha joined the Prime Minister's Rural Development Fellowship and moved to a left-wing extremist village in Jharkand to work on village development. He called Shaheen shortly after to say that he saw more clearly than ever how education was the only thing that could change lives. Prabhu Guthi and Indira Aditi-Rawat joined Room To Read, a non-profit organization with the vision of setting up libraries across government schools. Kishan Gopal went back to Tata Consultancy Services, determined to see how the corporate sector could support education. Surya Pratap and Kanika Saraff chose school leadership, and developed an idea that became the Reimagine Learning Community, a free, bi-lingual, democratic school in rural

Maharashtra. Their vision was to develop a school space that was on the vanguard of social change, empowering individuals to participate consciously and critically in society. Reimagine aimed to balance individual freedom and examine each child's role in nurturing the common good.

> *'Enter our learning community and you may find 3-year-old Aarti exercising her right to roam during class time and sitting by herself with a book by the tree, or our 4-year-olds seated in a circle addressing their collective issues during morning circle time. At playtime, if you happen to peep outside through our office window, you will see a universe of fun, imagination, and love. Sometimes it is difficult to spot the teacher from the child!'*
>
> —Surya Pratap, 2009 Teach For India Alumnus and Founder, Reimagine Learning Community

~

Teach For India started thinking more critically about the role the organization could play in accelerating each Alumnus's impact. Even the most driven Alumnus with the clearest vision graduated from the Fellowship into an overwhelmingly challenging environment. It was difficult to raise money, to find people, and to build culture. A conversation began around what it would take to truly drive systemic change. From a complex puzzle, whose pieces ranged from teacher training to media, a subset of priorities was now identified. Teach For India believed that solving these would quickly create proof points of excellence in areas central to achieving its vision. Among these priorities were teaching, teacher training, school leadership, and corporate social responsibility in education.

At the same time, Teach For India continued to believe that scale was vital to catalyzing change in the country. An expansion department was set up within the organization to explore potential new sites and work to get them set up. Chennai and Hyderabad would be the next in line to launch, and the recruitment team had an ambitious target of bringing in 7500 applications and 450 Fellows. Collective action was needed to meet this goal; Fellows and staff were given a 'Recruitment in a Box' package and a Find-a-Fellow scheme was launched to get Fellows to search for a replacement Fellow to teach their students after they left.

Srini Srinivasan would graduate from the Fellowship and move straight to Chennai as our first City Director.

'We were eagerly preparing for June 2012. I was managing the demands of the final months in my classroom and also the demands of setting up Teach for India in Chennai. I felt that I never managed to keep my head above the water—forever busy, excited, and exhausted but often very happy. Every day was a race against time. In the months leading to launching Teach For India in Chennai, I would remember K. Kamaraj, the leader who introduced the midday meal scheme in Tamil Nadu, for his far-reaching vision and love for children. My mother, who eventually dropped out of secondary school in Tamil Nadu, used to tell me that the aroma of hot dal and rice used to pull her to school every day and kept her from becoming a dropout.

> 'As we set up our office, we felt a mix of emotions—excitement, nervousness, joy, and also worry. The schools had been signed up, our Fellows were getting ready to teach at Institute, our children were ready to step in to their classrooms, and yet there was a lot left to be done. We wanted Teach For India in Chennai to have a 'tamizhmanam' (Tamil flavour) and yet retain the core culture that we shared across cities. We told ourselves that all of us would try to operate like entrepreneurs, taking individual ownership to build things, driven by a strong desire to see Chennai's children on the path to building their lives.'
>
> —Srini Srinivasan, 2010 Teach For India Alumnus and former Chennai City Director

Emily Dew relocated from the UK to work on Teach For India's programme team.

> 'And then it was time. The lush post-monsoon canopies covered the entire city, and each morning the little people of Chennai crossed the school gates, with smiles and solemn glances, colourful ribbons, neatly combed hair, and lovingly powdered cheeks accompanied by heavy tiffin baskets, ready for the day ahead and waiting to learn.'
>
> —Emily Dew, Senior Programme Manager, Teach For India

Chennai launched as a small family of 29 Fellows. More stories of learning unfolded, like Aravind Prasad's Class of

Champions and how they redefined safety for him.

> *'The rain outside has just ceased. It has stopped suddenly without a warning. Similarly, certain abrupt and unexpected events shape my students' lives. When they occur, my students want a shelter from the tougher realities of life. A realization that my classroom is that shelter is very humbling. My classroom needs to be full of life, love, and joy. It must evoke a sense of hope, just like the rain did this evening.'*

—Aravind Balagi Prasad, 2012 Teach For India Alumnus and Programme Manager, Schools Vertical, Central Square Foundation

While in the classroom next door to Aravind, Revathi Ramanan lives his story,

> *'Let me try and explain why teaching is the toughest job you can ever imagine. Imagine your best self. One that is happy, cheerful, forgiving, patient, loving, kind, generous, grateful, empathetic, focused. Now think of the number of days in a year that you actually are your best self. Think of the situations in which this best self usually comes out and the people with whom it is easiest for you to be your best self.*
>
> *'Well, here's the thing. If you are a teacher, you need to be your best self, every single day of the year. In a dark, leaking, cramped room, or a scorching, asbestos roofed shed that acts as a classroom. When a child throws a tantrum, or calls you names. Even when the roof of your*

classroom leaks in the middle of a lesson.

'My biggest learning as a teacher was this: children learn rigorous academic content from what you teach but they learn values from the person that you are. You can talk about grit all you want in the classroom, but the minute the children see you giving up on that one child in the classroom, they will give up too. You can talk about integrity and perseverance till your throat goes hoarse but you come late to school one day or you come to school without a plan and children will learn from that. You can talk about all the values in the world but unless your best self comes alive every single day, chances are that your children's best self isn't going to shine. That's why it is tough.'

—Revathi Ramanan, 2011 Teach For India Alumnus and Programme Manager, Teach For India

Despite all the many obstacles, significant change was visible across Chennai classrooms in under a year. Archana Iyer's 3rd standard students were discussing gender equality fluently, when just eight months earlier they couldn't speak a sentence in English. After Adhi Selvam graduated from the fellowship, his student Priya said, *'Adhi Sir used to not just teach me the subjects, he would also teach me about life and that I must also think about the society around me. I am going to continue learning those extra things on my own. I am going to be a writer and I am going to write down all of my thoughts about different things and try and understand them.'*

From its first year, the Chennai team worked to impact

through the existing system. Staff member Merlia Tanseer worked closely with T.N. Venkatesh, the Joint Commissioner of Education, who was motivated and excited about driving real change. He sent regular delegations of Corporation of Chennai teachers and School Principals to Mumbai and Pune, and to attend Teach For India's inspirED conferences. With his support, Teach For India also piloted a co-teaching model with government schoolteachers where a Fellow would teach alongside Corporation of Chennai schoolteachers. Teach For India Fellow practices came to life as government schoolteachers started using word walls, singing phonics songs, and giving their students high-fives. Effective teaching practices were shared at conferences in Chennai where all Corporation School Principals were invited to come and learn together, and were welcomed with Firkis by Teach For India children. They sat in small groups with Fellows to discuss the vision they had for their schools, and watched students read out essays on social justice. An open forum created the space for Principals to share challenges openly, and the days ended with personal notes of gratitude.

~

Srini was in his last year of teaching and at the same time set up the Chennai branch while Saahil spent a year in Hyderabad preparing for Teach For India's Hyderabad launch. In Hyderabad, Teach For India was received with warmth and excitement. Four thousand low-income private schools mushroomed across the city, born out of a strong parental demand for good quality, English-medium education. The Principals of these schools were extremely receptive to Teach For India; they were accustomed to an already thriving ecosystem of organizations across the city working in the area of education. The bureaucracy was equally motivated, and would give Teach For India its first government funding through the Vidya Volunteer Scheme in which a small part of each Fellow's stipend was covered by the government.

> 'Hyderabad started off with a team of 55 people; 47 Fellows and 8 staff members. All 55 of us were doing this for the first time in our lives. In our first year, we would need to figure out the schools, communities, and the city. During one of our first few days in Hyderabad, we were thrown out of a classroom because the school was a designated centre for the Board exams. We had nowhere to teach. As if it was the obvious thing to do, our Fellows calmly started teaching on a small run-down piece of blackboard in the school field. This ownership characterized our team that first year.'
>
> — Saahil Sood, 2009 Teach For India Alumnus, former City Director, Hyderabad and City Director, Ahmedabad

Soon after their arrival, Hyderabad Fellows came face-to-face with the Telangana riots and communal tension where hordes of rioters stormed violently into the school where Fellows Priyanka Mohan and Shalini Pathi taught, and they calmly told their students to leave and come back later that afternoon. In a couple of hours the students were back, refocused, inside a shuttered classroom.

When Aadi Rungta moved from Mumbai to teach in the Old City, one of his students asked whether he prayed the Namaz. When Aadi said he was a Hindu and didn't the student found this unacceptable, and would no longer speak to his teacher. Early community visits were often awkward; a student's mother stood concealed behind a curtain and would not answer him when he spoke. Along with co-Fellows Vikrant Patro and Umashankar Reddy, Aadi started a community centre at the school replete with a library, board games, an audio-visual section and e-learning tools. This centre would keep the children in school for 8-9 hours of the day. In eight months, the change was apparent. The credibility that Vikrant, Uma, and Aadi built with their students resulted in them being welcomed into the very same homes by the mothers who had once rejected them.

The Hyderabad team was able to recreate a culture of deep ownership, not just in Fellows but in their families as well. In a training session with the Fellows' families a mother stated that seeing the important work that her daughter and son-in-law were doing, she, now wakes daily at 5 am to prepare breakfast and lunch for them. In turn her husband would now arise at 4:45 to make tea for his wife. There were several parents who talked about the many changes they were seeing in their children. One man spoke of how he became worried when his wife Kriti started speaking another man's name in her sleep, until he realized, somewhat foolishly, that it was the name of one of her struggling students.

Drastic transformation occurred in Hyderabad over the short period of two years, both in the classroom and across communities. Shivani Gandhi, Hyderabad's Senior Programme Manager, walked into Fellow Jagdish's classroom when he first started teaching. 'His 45 innocent looking kids stared at him with 100 percent attention for exactly 30 seconds, before hell broke loose. My heart melted as I saw Jagdish stand there and say "1-2-3 eyes on *me*", for the 8th time in 8 minutes. I particularly remember Ishaaq, a blue-eyed child in the class, who would have periodic fits of rage. When I walked in a year later, I wondered if I was in the same class. All the kids, including Ishaaq, were silently engaged in reading a poem, inferring about character's feelings and thinking independently.'

So many low-income private school Principals were also eager for change. They would push Fellows to run workshops for their teachers and encourage them to share effective practices. School Principal Conferences run by Teach For India staff got close to 98 percent attendance. Principals and teachers travelled to inspirED conferences in Pune and Mumbai, and then marvelously insisted that Teach For India host an inspirED Hyderabad conference. In 2013, inspirED Hyderabad brought together 400 educators from across Hyderabad. They came together at the beautiful campus of ISB, and participants were awed by the way Pushkar Joshi's 4th standard girls talked to them about female infanticide. Sapna Shah's students exhibited the truth of their daily lives using photographs, and Santosh Prasad's students spoke about their 'Be the Change Project' where 8th standard children in his school were being mentored by older students in the community.

Mohammed Anwar, the Principal of the M.A. Ideal chain of low-income schools in Hyderabad, described the changes in his schools as a changed thinking process and clarity of vision, increased ownership of the school by his teachers, use of new teaching methodology to increase student confidence. He was determined to give *every* child in his community a quality education within the budget that the school had.

Hyderabad was now a hub of education reform, and with school Principals, teachers, parents, and a growing number of organizations focused as partners with the common task of equity and excellence in education. In these pieces coming together, Hyderabad was now poised for significant impact.

Teach For India was now reaching 16,216 children across 164 schools.

~

To better prepare Alumni for the path beyond the Fellowship, Teach For India fleshed out a leadership framework for Fellows. Its model was in the shape of a Firki. At the centre of the Firki were Teach For India's core values, which now included Excellence and Seva. Teaching as Leadership Principles encircled the core values. The spokes of the Firki were the four Fellow goals: impact on self, class, school/community, and country. Fellows were introduced to the idea that Teach For India's core values and goals, and the 'Teaching as Leadership' principles added up to transformational teaching *and* leadership. They would spend two years becoming the kind of leaders who would work to put *all* children on a different life path.

Externally, Teach For India needed to be actively involved in the dialogue around education reform; to develop partnerships with the government to figure out what policy changes and which resources could drive change in the quality of teaching. Delhi was an avenue for Teach For India to begin to engage not just with local government around school placement, but also with the Central government. Shaheen was invited to join a committee overseeing the National Council For Teacher Education (NCTE), a national level body for teacher education across India. Over the next two years, the Committee worked to push for higher quality teacher education, review teacher education curriculum, and rewrite the regulations and procedures for becoming a recognized teacher education institute.

Kapil Sibal, the then Minister HRD, became a supporter of Teach For India after interacting with Fellows and staff at a dinner in Delhi hosted for Teach For India by Richard Stagg, the then British High Commissioner. He would speak often of the power of young people in changing education. His successor, Mallipudi Mangapati Pallam Raju, taught in a Teach For India classroom and tweeted, 'It was a fun experience to share the joyful environment of grade three, and to observe the positive impact of the Teach For India Fellows on the little girls. Since a substantial number of Teach For India Fellows are motivated towards teaching, a solution must be found to bring them into the profession.'

Delhi's first inspirED conference brought together hundreds of educators and other stakeholders. The conference had 'Sense of Possibility' as its theme, and offered participants a range of sessions across three tracks: classroom, school, and systemic change. On the beautiful campus of Delhi's Vasant Valley School the energy was palpable: little children taught Yoga to visiting delegates, a vibrant education exhibition manned by students showed examples of creative learning, and pop-up street plays that focused on important social issues. Mike Feinberg, Teach For America Alumnus and the founder of KIPP talked about his journey of creating a hundred schools for children from low-income families in the US, in partnership with the government. Rohit Dhankar, the Founder of Digantar, a school in rural Rajasthan, spoke to a packed audience about the history and evolution of education in India. Steven Farr, Teach For All's Chief Knowledge Officer and the architect of Teaching As Leadership did an eye-opening session on what transformational teaching actually is.

Jon Schnur, Founder of America Achieves and New Leaders For New Schools, and Obama's education advisor came back to India for his second inspirED conference, sharing his journey in education and belief in the role that policy can play to bring about change. Jon was one of the kindest, gentlest, most humble leaders Shaheen had encountered. He talked to everyone, with his body leaned forward to fully concentrate on the words of every child, parent, and teacher that he met. On a school visit a little girl named Jabeez ran up to Jon and Shaheen. Jabeez lived in an orphanage, and had wanted to meet Shaheen to ask her how she, one day, could join Teach For India. Jabeez asked Jon question after question: who he knew, what he did, how he selected and trained educators, what it would take to help kids. Jon would return to the US and write a poem inspired by Jabeez and the children of India.

*'When you meet a child of India,
And see their smiles,
What will you tell them,
You've done to help across the miles?*

*When you meet a child of India,
And see a future flower,
What will you tell them,
You have done with your power?*

*So what do I think,
Of this present they gave?
The children of India,
Show me how to be brave.'*

At a local level, Shaheen had begun conversations during her time at Akanksha about the need for private participation in municipal schools, and the PPP policy was starting to seem like it would become a reality in Mumbai. At a national level, with the Right to Education (RTE) Act, it seemed like alternative teacher certification was critical to improving the quality of teachers in India. This would encourage a wider pool of driven, qualified people to enter teaching, holding the bar as high or even higher than the current standards required for teacher certification.

~

Inspired by the examples set for them, Fellows too, were pushing the bar. Nallika Braganza and Antara Ashra's 4th standard students started an 'Inspire Passion Project', and performed *Final Solutions*, a play by Mahesh Dattani about Hindu-Muslim communal tension. The children spent months dissecting and analyzing the complex script, writing the back stories for the characters, and creating lighting, costume, and prop solutions. The show came together in an astounding example of the power of the arts in education.

Adithya Narayanan and Mary Dominic set up a football team for their boys, until one day a student asked Adithya, 'Bhaiya, why not a girls' football team?' The community he taught in was conservative, even dance was not encouraged for girls, and football completely unheard of. They started anyway, and six months later, the girls played against the boys in a match and won 6-0.

'That day, I realized that football had taught them something about gender equality that the community may have never taught them. To my girls now, gender isn't a criteria, it's not an advantage or a disadvantage that you're born with. The match introduced them to the idea that they could do anything that the boys could. This experience gave a sense of independence and self-belief to my girls.'

—Adithya Narayanan, 2012 Teach For India Alumnus and Mumbai Alumni Impact Manager, Teach For India

When Ashwath Bharath entered the Fellowship, he wanted to ensure that his 5th standard students were prepared to enter the 21st century as productive citizens, and centred his classroom on the theme of 'city-building'. He brought tablet computers into his classroom, and thereby empowered his students to teach each other math. On any given day, students would be planning an imaginary town in Civics, thinking through the history and culture of the city in Social Studies, or calculating the distances of the roads in Math. At the end of the year, they built and presented their model city, but they also surpassed the national average on the rigorous Asset Examination, an exam taken almost entirely by students at high-performing, high-income private schools.

Classroom stories sparked joy, and what was truly impressive was what Fellows ventured to do after the Fellowship. Saurabh Taneja struggled as a teacher during his first year; his secondary school students seemed to have perfected bad behaviour as years of disinterest in education caught up with them. To see where he was three years after he graduated from the Fellowship was testimony to the belief that dramatic change happens.

> 'My first couple of months of teaching were a rude awakening. I had read about inequity but now it was starkly staring me in the face. How could I find the time and bandwidth to impact my students in the way I wanted to? Fast forward to year two, and another stark reality hit me. Our school ended at class 7; my kids wouldn't have a school to go to after this year. That's when I knew that I wanted to focus on secondary school. It didn't make sense that we had 10 percent the number of secondary schools as compared to primary. What would happen to those kids?
>
> 'After the Fellowship, I joined a start-up girls' leadership academy that never quite took off, then worked in Jaipur with Bodh, a non-profit working on wide-scale

teacher training, all the while holding this dream of starting a school. At the same time, Teach For India and Akanksha were wrestling with the same challenge I had faced in my school in Pune. Pune didn't have a single English-medium government secondary school; all our Teach For India 7th standard students were at risk of dropping out. We worked to convince the government until they allowed us to set up, and run, Pune's first English-medium government secondary school, and I relocated to start the school. Our team had a daunting task of getting children, many of whom were at a grade 3 level to graduate from class 10 — in less than 420 instructional days. School leadership is very, very hard. It's hard to keep a team inspired through incredibly long days and a far-reaching goal. It's hard to live up to our school name, the School Of Leaders, knowing that values and leadership need to be lived by us each day. But the magnitude of the challenge and the importance of what we are trying to do keeps me focused on what is important.'

—Saurabh Taneja, 2009 Teach For India Alumnus and School Leader, Acharya Vinoba Bhave School

The colours of the Teach For India movement had never been so bright. Shaheen would write in another email to Fellows and the staff:

'Over the past years, there have been many times when I've wavered from my own sense of possibility. When I've really stopped and needed to look in the mirror and say — Is this possible? Can we really be at the forefront of making 50

years happen? Can the children I see in every classroom really get on that different life path that we know is so important for them? These questions often make me nervous, sometimes they even make me feel guilty. But luckily, whenever I encounter moments of doubt, they pass. They pass not because of a crazy idealistic notion that this is possible (though I have that too) — they pass because of the evidence that we're accruing in our classrooms. They pass because of the empirical data we've accumulated, from story after story, on the real transformation that is the result of our Alumni's efforts. They pass because I see how driven our staff team is to get to that place of equity and excellence — 50 years from now.'

∼

The Teach For All Network continued to provide knowledge and inspiration to Teach For India. Eric Scroggins, Teach For America's Bay Area Executive Director, visited India and helped the Teach For India team to understand the value of regionalization and the creation of City Visions. Now cities themselves began to ask the question, 'What will it take to get an excellent education to all children?' They would start mapping out the city education landscape, look for opportunities in their city, and identify the positions from which Alumni could have the most significant impact.

Teach For America's Steven Farr continued to be the greatest thought partner on anything to do with the classroom. Inspired by Teach For America's Sue Lehman Award that recognized transformational teaching, Teach For

India created the Transformational Impact Journey. The Transformational Impact Journey searched for classrooms that could best answer 'Yes' to the question 'Will students walk out of this classroom on a fundamentally different life path, with greater opportunity, and choice in life?' When the idea of the award was introduced there was much dissent. Fellows believed such an award was inherently unfair and would promote competition. An email to all went out with the subject line, 'Say **no** to the transformational impact award'. The team considered the Fellow's grievances and reimagined the award as a journey with a re-explained purpose:

> *'The Transformational Impact Journey has been defined by one underlying belief: We have the most to learn from each other, from the countless examples of excellence that are produced, every single day, from each of you.'*

—Sandeep Rai, City Director, Pune, Teach For India

A year later, the Transformational Impact Journey came to life. In its first year, 70 teachers were nominated and invaluable artifacts that included lesson plans, vision statements, classroom footage, and resources were collected. Adhishree Parasnis, Teach For India Pune's HR and Alumni Manager, went around the country capturing video footage of the nominated classrooms, and came back with many stories. A process of intense discussion and inquiry led to the selection of Nirali Vasisht, Archana Iyer, and Sapna Shah's classrooms.

'The bell rang for recess and the class broke into the customary scuffle. My friend who had agreed to document our most inspiring classrooms busied himself with the equipment as I helped. Shivani stood by the door watching our every move. "Akka," says Shivani finally, "is Anna your best friend?" Completely caught off guard I reply, "He's a good friend. We went to college together. Do you have a best friend?" Shivani runs out the door and returns with Saniya. "Akka! This is my bestest friend Saniya." They both break into giggles and swing their clasped hands. "That's wonderful! Shivani, what makes Saniya your bestest friend?" I ask. After recovering from another bout of giggling, Shivani looks at Saniya and then back at me with wide eyes. "Akka, why because Saniya and I are bench partners here and will be in college also. Also our values are same-same. Hard work and respecting elders. Bestest friends have same values. Your values are matching with Anna's?"'

—Adhishree Parasnis, 2011 Teach For India Alumnus and Pune City HR and Alumni Manager, Teach For India

Similar conversations were happening in Teach For All partner countries around the world. Conferences in Chile and China provided rich dialogue around the meaning of transformation, Alumni impact and systemic reform across the world. Shaheen was among 300 people from across the Teach For All network who visited China together. While there, they watched a video of Teach For America Alumnus Michael Johnston, who was now a State Senator in Colorado, and spoke of his time as Principal of a failing school. Fifty percent of children in his school failed to graduate from school every year. On his first day, he told his students that all of them would go to a four-year college of their choice with the scholarship money to get there. One can only imagine the excitement that erupted as the school was assembled in the gym on the day that the last child, Travis, received his admission letter to college. Michael ended saying that Teach For America for him had been a great lesson in truth and hope; *truth without hope was failure and hope without truth was fantasy.*

Truth and Hope resonated deeply. It would become a key way in which Teach For India would define itself in the years to come. The truth was that India had 200 million children of school-going age to educate. The hope was that it was possible to accomplish this, and with excellence. The truth could be disturbing, scary, overwhelming. And with hope, there was nothing that could not be done.

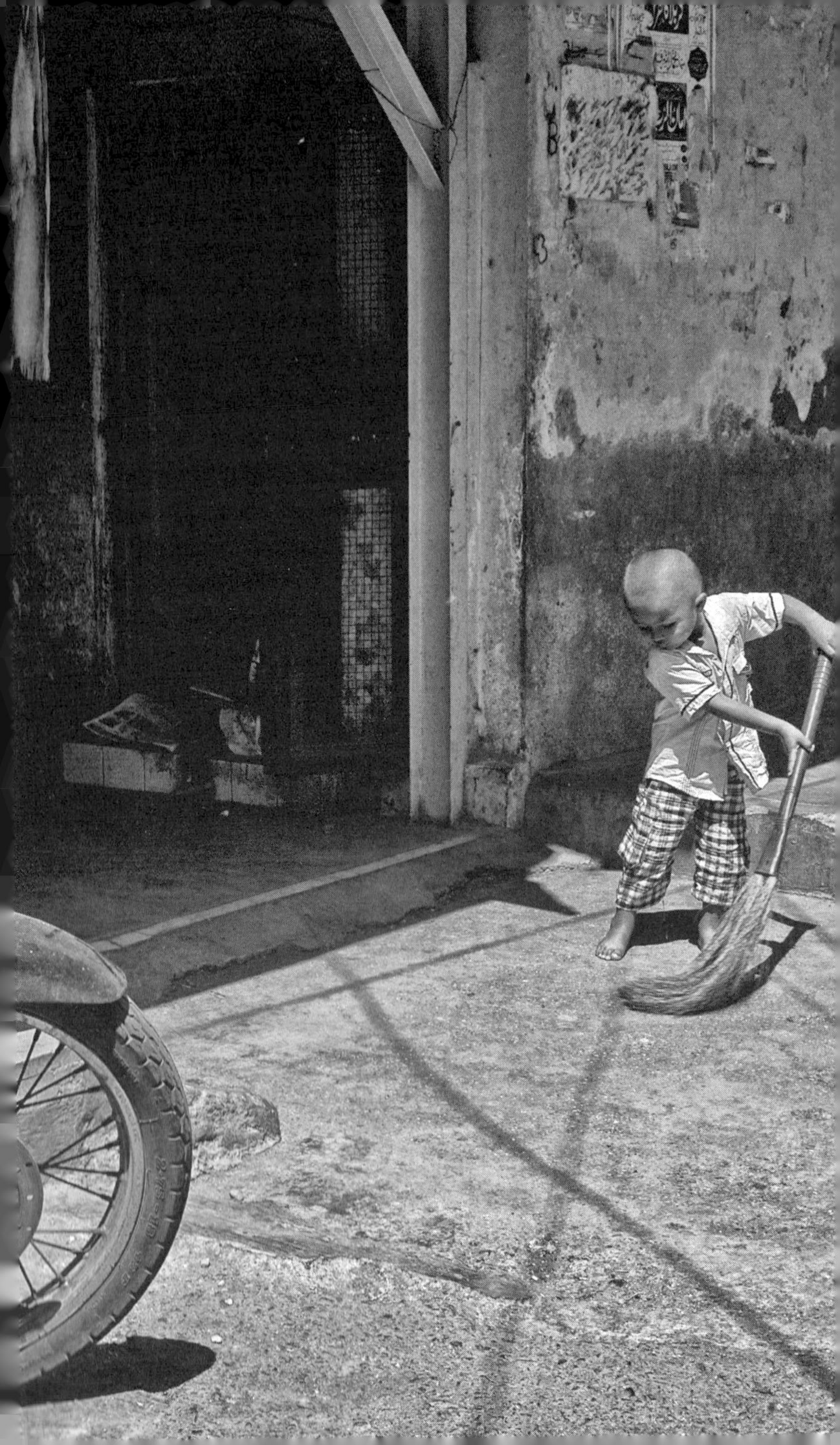

CHAPTER 10

SEVA

'Didi, can I ask you a question?'
'Yes, of course.'
'Can you use two conjunctions side by side in one sentence?'
'Why don't you tell us how to?'
'Life is beautiful, and so are you.'
'Wow, who taught you that?'
'My teacher, Dipti Didi. She says this to us every day.'

—Khushi

The Gandhi Ashram, right in the middle of Ahmedabad, has a small museum filled with photographs of Gandhiji as well as texts with many of his quotes and writings. One of those photographs has this simple picture of his wooden slippers and a quote, which reads:

'I am mostly busy making sandals these days. I have already made about 15 pairs. When you need new ones now, please send me the measurements. And when you do so, mark the places where the strap is to be fixed—that is on the outer side of the big toe and the little one.'

The idea that impact is driven by small acts of kindness is the life force behind Teach For India; and is an idea that came to Shaheen through a simple man in Ahmedabad named Jayesh Patel, and fondly known to all as Jayeshbhai. Shaheen met Jayeshbhai fifteen years ago when she and Rajshree led a group of Akanksha students on a trip to the Sabarmati Ashram. Jayeshbhai beamed every time he spoke of his father, Ishwarbhai, and would lovingly touch the face of his statue each morning as he walked past it. You could observe him in that moment as a little boy and witness the close connection between this intensely special father and son. Affectionately, Jayeshbhai tells the story of how when he was nine years old his father asked for him to get down on his knees, and alongside him clean over a hundred filthy and putrid overfilled public toilets. Ishwarbhai, born a Brahmin, had gone to Gandhiji and asked where he could be most effective in India's struggle for independence and survival. Gandhiji had given him the responsibility of sanitation, recognizing the power and passion Ishwarbhai could give to this fundamental and central issue that was essential to the very survival of the nation. Ishwarbhai was fondly called the 'toilet king', and Jayeshbhai grew up with the embarrassing title 'baby toilet', which he now proclaimed with sheer glee. There was real power in his humility. Ishwarbhai wanted his son to realize that no job was below him and to experience the true dignity of labour. Ishwarbhai believed that when one bent to sweep the dirt outside one would simultaneously purify oneself internally. Jayeshbhai would devote a lifetime building on his father's vision of sanitation, personal transformation, and love.

They were simple experiences that Shaheen had with Jayeshbhai, many of which left an indelible impression on her. It was morning as the children entered the Gandhi Ashram, and they were asked to take off their slippers. As children will, they left them chaotically strewn all over the verandah. Jayeshbhai, simply smiled and bent down to pick up each slipper, arranging them in a neat line of matching pairs. After running around the garden during recess, the children re-entered the Ashram and once again threw their slippers into an unruly pile. Without saying a word and still, with the sincerest smile, Jayeshbhai bent again to arrange them. The following morning when the kids entered the Ashram, they meticulously placed their slippers in a neat row, just as they had been when Jayeshbhai arranged them the day before. No one had reprimanded the children or even said anything to them, they had been led by example. This was a simple and direct lesson on how to have maximum impact, a living example of Gandhiji's words 'Be the change you wish to see in the world'.

Sometimes in the summer Gujarat seemed to be melting, and Jayeshbhai and Shaheen were stopped at a traffic light when a few children ran to the window. Jayeshbhai lovingly invited them to thrust their faces in front of the airconditioner. The children burst into peals of happy laughter, relishing the clean cool air on their overheated faces. Was this a momentary fix or did it really make a difference? 'For that moment, they were happy', he said. 'That matters'.

> *'Something simple that affected me a lot on those early trips was the circle of confession that Jayeshbhai would lead. He would start with himself, making himself vulnerable, and then we would all share. The circle acknowledged that we are all human beings striving to be better. Jayeshbhai taught me to do simple things. Do I tell my maid that she is a blessing to me? I travel a lot and leave my home to her; I could not do it without her. Does she know how important she is to me?'*
>
> —Rajshree Doshi, former Akanksha teacher and Coach, Akanksha and Teach For India

It was clear that while achievements were important, it was the journey of 'love made visible' that had ultimate significance. In a speech with Fellows several months later, Shaheen explained her vision for this principle:

> *'Think of little things in the context of our classrooms. How every smile, every observation of every child, every lesson plan, every question, every visit to a child's home — how each of the million "every's" can be so precious in themselves. There is magic in the lesson plan that comes to life. There is magic in the courage it takes for a child to make a mistake. There is magic that happens when a child picks up the phone to call and ask for help with a Math sum he or she has for homework.'*

~

As a result of the time Shaheen spent with Jayeshbhai and all her rich experiences at the Gandhi Ashram, Teach For India eventually added 'Seva' as one of its core values.

> *'"To give and to receive joyfully" reads the Teach For India core value definition of Seva. I stop to think about exactly what this sentence means to me at this point in time, in my life. You see, that's the beauty of our interactions with our values at Teach For India; each of them are redefined as we experience new things, each value acquires new meaning, it's almost as if they reinvent themselves to suit the various incarnations we adopt along our journey in this movement.'*
>
> —Anasuya Menon, 2009 Teach For India Alumnus and Personal Leadership Coach, Teach For India

Shaheen would return to Ahmedabad repeatedly, taking students, colleagues, friends, and family. Over time, she began to better understand this incredible ecosystem of small (and large) acts of kindness, and its incalculable ripples, that Jayeshbai had effected. Raghubhai, who was afflicted by polio and paralysed from the waist down, left his village as a child because he deeply worried that his parents just couldn't afford to care for him. Arriving in Mumbai, he sat outside one of the local Gurudwaras, minding people's sandals as they took them off to enter the mosque. A volunteer encountered him there and was struck by his joyful face and the sincerity with which he arranged the sandals in straight lines, and immediately brought him to Jayeshbhai back to Ahmedabad. Raghubhai would later buy a hands-only cycle, which he used to start an unusual venture called Tyaag Nu Tiffin, a business that delivered over 30 tiffin lunches daily to elderly ladies in the community. It didn't stop there. When Raghubhai heard of trouble in community homes, he would take a Tulsi plant and gift it as an offering of peace. Tragically, Raghubhai was killed in an accident when a speeding truck ran over his hand-cycle.

Anjali Desai had grown up in the US, and now ran a school for street children in Ahmedabad that she had built along with her students with their bare hands, using recycled materials. If you entered the school and you'd see the proudest children ever, watering their plants in a little garden, dusting off the little place of worship they had created, or sitting in a circle, listening to a story on values. When asked what the most important thing in the world was, the children's unhesitating first answer was 'love'.

Across town, Udaybhai operated a rickshaw that was beautifully decorated with inspirational quotes on a pay-it-forward system. Rides in his rickshaw would be accompanied by wonderful stories, and perhaps most surprisingly a meter that always stayed at zero. If you did want to pay, Udaybhai would use it on the person taking the rickshaw after you. He had run his rickshaw like this for years now, able to support his wife and children on the power of his faith in love and fairness.

Anand Shah and his two sisters started Indicorps, a Fellowship programme that brought Indian Americans back to India to immerse themselves in often arduous, year-long, personal transformation service projects. Years after Indicorps inception, Anand would be one of the first people to inspire the creation of Teach For India. There was Sureshbhai, who would go into hundreds of villages to mobilize the community around issues of sanitation and women's rights. There was Gopal Dada, a Shanti Sainak and an ardent follower of social reformer Vinobha Bhave, who had spent years spreading messages of peace and generosity across the villages of India. Until the day before he passed away at the age of 87, Gopal Dada would wake up at 4 am and sing bhajans to simply spread joy, along with a myriad variety of birds on his morning walk at dawn. A progressive, far ahead of his time, he had delighted in seeing the work of Jayeshbhai, whom he had seen grow from a child to inspire so many others.

It was impossible to estimate the impact that emanated from the way Jayeshbhai lived his life. Without any formal goals, with no 'marketing' whatsoever, thousands of people would come and visit him, and always leave feeling transformed.

There was Nipun, who spent a year walking in India along with wife Guri, spending less than a dollar a day between them. They chose instead to trust in the power of love to take care of them. They lived their lives doing small acts of service.

Nimesh Patel, or 'Nimo', left his life and promising career in Los Angeles as a rapper in the popular group Karmacy to work with children from a slum community in Ahmedabad on a musical called Ekatva, or unity. Nimo's children would end up touring the US and Europe, and by the end of the performances, he would choose to remain in Ahmedabad, writing a different kind of music now—music that would lift children's hearts and thereby change the world. Nimo's songs 'Grateful' and 'Being Kind' would become the anthems of the Institute and Teach For India event, and would form part of his album 'Empty Hands'. Nimo had an instantaneous way of connecting with children. After conducting a workshop on kindness with a group of Teach For India students, 14-year-old Priyanka sent him a letter:

Dear Nimo Bhaiyya,

I am Priyanka, you don't know me, but I know you because you are on my inspiration list. You don't know it but your life has been a great inspiration for me. I know your life story; through it I learnt that our life should be for others. I will definitely change the lives of people who are suffering from a deadly disease—the disease of living in this world but still being dead. This is not a disease caused by a virus or bacteria; it is caused by the deficiency

*of humanity. I don't know how many lives I'll be able to
transform but I am sure a small step can change a lot.*

*Love,
Priyanka*

Nimo wanted to figure out how to support Priyanka, in Jayeshbhai's language, how to be her 'ladder'. He sent her a plane ticket to travel to Ahmedabad to a 'Moved by Love' retreat. Moved by Love was a term first used by Vinobha Bhave, the social reformer who had walked for thirteen years across India appealing to rich landowners to give away their land to the poor. It was the largest ever transfer of land in history with no commercial exchange whatsoever. Vinobhaji's simple strategy was to ask each landowner to think of him as though he were a son and therefore give him 1/6 of his land which he would in turn sign over to poor farmers.

The Moved by Love retreats brought together people from all over the world to explore and experience the idea of human inter-connectedness and care. Priyanka travelled to Ahmedabad on her first flight, accompanied by her teddy bear, Nia, who had been the sole constant fixture in her otherwise traumatic life. At the retreat, Priyanka spent three days engaged in acts of service and shared stories from her own life. And in return, the attendants showered her with love. A few weeks later, Priyanka was in Mumbai at a live-in facility for homeless elderly people. Priyanka's teacher, Sanaya, asked the children to 'connect' with any of the elderly people, and Priyanka found herself with Krishna Vellu, an old lady who couldn't speak any language that she knew. She could easily have found another person, one who spoke a common language. But Priyanka chose instead to use actions, hugs, and smiles to communicate with Krishna for the 90-minute visit.

A few weeks later, the children were back in Mumbai and keen to go back to the home. Priyanka was excited to meet Krishna again, and brought a chocolate to give her. Priyanka approached Krishna, carrying Nia, as always, and gave her the chocolate. Krishna looked up, not seeing the chocolate, and thought Priyanka had brought *Nia* to give to her, and smiled delightedly as she held out her hands to receive the bear. Priyanka was torn. Should she try and explain what Nia meant to her, or should she give away what she believed to be her only real security? Priyanka looked at the lady's old smiling face, eyes affixed on hers, so happy to see this child she didn't know, who had come from nowhere, bringing life and love. Priyanka met her gaze, and smiling back, gave Nia away.

In 2012, Shaheen took her brother Rishad to Ahmedabad to meet Jayeshbhai. Along with Sureshbhai and a Gandhian scholar from Japan who was also visiting, they went to see an ancient well where they encountered a group of school children on a school trip. As the students walked by, Jayeshbhai tapped some of them on the head. Others he touched on the shoulder, with still others he energetically shook hands with, laughingly introducing himself. The students eventually crowded around and were enthralled, as he told jokes in funny voices, and talked to them about the importance of clipping their nails. He led them in a cheer against keeping trash in the house, 'kachra – *bahar!*' As they dispersed, he bent down and started picking up the garbage around him. In groups, the children joined in, picking up any garbage that *they* saw around *them*. Within fifteen minutes, the whole field around Jayeshbhai, which was previously strewn with garbage, was now spotlessly clean. Each one of those kids would return to their homes thinking about India's need for sanitation. More than that, they now realized that they could actually make a difference. India could be a clean and beautiful place.

Through the direct, loving, and humorous nature of his approach, Jayeshbhai would immediately establish a real rapport with strangers, like that with a close friend or family member. He repeatedly stopped young men on the road and appealed for them to quit smoking. He often referred to these strangers, in conversation, as his brothers, and proclaimed that he simply could not stand idly by and watch them kill themselves. Willingly, albeit reluctantly, they gave up their precious packs of bundled cigarettes that he would gleefully break in half. Jayeshbhai stopped to chat with a small old woman, her spine straight as iron, carrying a huge ceramic jug on her head. Jayeshbhai promptly lifted it off her head and put it atop Shaheen's brother's. He was 6'3', lived in New York, and was obviously the product of comfortable living and good nutrition. 'See how heavy?' Jayeshbhai exclaimed.

A group of private school girls in uniform were walking by and Jayeshbhai drew them into the group that had now formed on the street, each taking turns placing the heavy jug on their respective heads. He wanted them to test the weight and laugh, to all together marvel at the strength of the old woman. In that single moment, Jayeshbhai brought together people of different social classes, from across nations, languages and age groups there on the side of the dusty road in Ahmedabad, just to laugh for a second and learn from experiencing a sense of oneness, and indeed, love.

Jayeshbhai repeatedly explained the significance of his way of life to Shaheen's brother, sometimes through a series of Gandhiji's quotes. 'When the 'i' becomes small, the eyes become wide open,' he would proudly explain. He talked of the oneness of all religions, explained the danger of ritual without true realization, and said that one must first light a candle in one's heart before lighting one in a church, mosque, or temple. He talked of the power of empathy and love, about how true strength lay in the ability to love your aggressor, to the point of choosing to endure injury over inflicting it. Jayeshbhai was a living example of the source from which Gandhiji himself had drawn his power. A man of small stature who, without many possessions other than his few pens and paper, who from his tiny wooden desk on the floor would lead India to win her independence overcoming all of the industry, all the legions of armies, battleships, and castles that comprised the economic and military might of the British Empire.

That late afternoon Jayeshbhai took the small group to visit master sculptor Kanthi Patel at his studio. On the walk there the group, now naturally and of their own accord, began picking up rubbish along the side of the road and marvelled at an enchanted lot of low trees where in the dappled shadows peacocks pranced.

It was a precious privilege to be in the presence of Kanthikaka who was now 87 years old, and who had spent more than 50 years sculpting the freedom fighters of India's Independence movement, which he always gifted to cities.

His marble and bronze heroes stood strong and humble in parks and places of prominence all around the world. At Kanthikaka's request, and much to the amusement of many a passer-by, Rishad would go home to New York and give the bronze statue of Gandhiji that stands in Union Square Park a big hug, tying a bracelet around his wrist given to him by Jayeshbhai in support of equal rights for village women in Gandhiji's own state of Gujarat.

As the number of Fellows grew, it was no longer logistically possible to take everyone to Ahmedabad. The team needed to find a place that could recreate the magic that Shaheen had found there.

> *'I was scared. This was my first year handling Personal Leadership for all cities, and I was one person planning not just one but three retreats. I remember feeling overwhelmed, like I had too much to handle and wasn't sure if I could do it. And then, I thought about our country. There just had to be so many other amazing things happening that we didn't even know about.'*
>
> —Anasuya Menon, 2009 Teach For India Alumnus and Personal Leadership Coach, Teach For India

The team finally narrowed the search down to a few special places. Anandwan, Baba Amte's community rehabilitation centre for leprosy patients and the disabled. Gandhiji's Sevagram Ashram and the Nai Taleem school that had been set up by him there. The Barefoot College, a non-profit founded by Bunker Roy to make rural communities self-sufficient, and the last was Auroville, a universal township aimed at realizing human unity. Fellows spoke to illiterate village grandmothers at Barefoot College who made solar panels and cookers, and watched the Barefoot Children's parliament in session. Where young children were making big decisions relating to education, water, and the environment. They watched how a community could live with dignity and self-sufficiency at a home for leprosy patients, and observed children learn that education was a blend of head, hand, and heart at the Nai Taleem School. They reflected on what community actually meant at Auroville, learnt from the experimental teaching methodologies at the Aurovillian schools, and engaged with the local communities. These were experiences that pushed Fellows and staff way beyond their comfort zones, which inspired awe, and left them feeling something inside them had changed. Anasuya would excitedly tell the team:

> *'India has so much to offer in her infinite wisdom; Teaching For India would require learning from her as well.'*

~

Teach For India now began to think about all of its core values—a Sense of Possibility, Resourcefulness, Respect and Humility, Excellence, Seva, Teamwork, and Reflection—as being linked by the larger idea of Love. Love made one believe deeply that things were possible. It ensured that we treated the object of our love as our most precious resource. Love enabled one to respect and value others equally and as equal to ourselves. Love pushed one to strive for excellence.

Love created a desire to serve and helped one navigate to do the right thing. Love made people work together as a family. When one loved, one reflected, always trying to become better. Loving oneself, and each other would get us to our vision of 50 years; a vision where all children would attain an excellent education.

Professional development changed. Staff participated in a 24-hour walk across Ahmedabad, where the directive was to think about the idea of faith. Jayeshbhai gathered the group in a circle on the sand outside his beloved toilet garden to wish them before they set off. An old, smiling, slightly senile toy-seller walked past and Jayeshbhai called him into the circle, welcoming him with pats on the back. The toy-seller gifted a plastic green parrot on little wheels to the group. It was a blistering day and the group set off to embrace the uncertainty that lay ahead. At a temple they stopped and laughed with a group of large langurs that were sitting around an old Banyan tree. At a mosque they learnt from a young woman the customary way to wash oneself before entering. Sureshbhai led them into the old city, and told them of his decision to eat one meal a day because he didn't need more, and of how he woke up every day now to pray, meditate, sing, and read something inspirational, all before the sun rose.

Nimo, who accompanied the City Directors and Shaheen, described the experience.

'We took the City Directors on a pad yatra, or a walking pilgrimage. This had no direct relevance to the work Teach For India does, but Shaheen saw that nurturing the internal process was important. We went into the

Old City in Ahmedabad without money or phones, just walking. By night, we were hungry, and thought we may need to sit and beg. We were in front of a fruit stall, and started talking to the vendor. As soon as we did, he offered to treat us to a full dinner, pulling money out of his wallet. Twelve of us were taken to a nearby little restaurant and fed a full meal. This man knew nothing about us except that we were hungry. The reflections were interesting; there was questioning on how this happened, on whether we should take from someone who had less than us, on what it meant to learn to receive. Sidharth left the day wondering whether he needed to leave Teach For India to understand the inner conflict he was feeling about spirituality. He was asking himself really hard questions: How do you love and remain detached? How do you strive to meet an impossible goal without getting obsessed by it?

'Too late now to find a place to sleep, we decided to sleep on the road. There were other homeless people sleeping next to us, some doing drugs. People called out from cars, and honked loudly. There were flies and mosquitoes. It was a night of dealing with our individual insecurities. That next morning we woke and walked home, awed by what had just happened. Each of us was a new person in his or her own way. In surrendering, we had elevated our faith. The world conspires to help you when you do something with faith and intention.'

—Nimesh Patel

Ahmedabad was a peacock that would leave his place on the highest tree to come when Jayeshbhai called him to eat out of our open hands. It was an imposing langur being shooed away by the bravery of a cawing crow, or a gentle cow belly-down, chewing undisturbed in the midst of the busiest traffic. One could join an inter-faith meditation or walk into the toilet café, where showerheads were converted into lights, and all different types of toilet bowls served now as café stools! One could see Anar Ben's organization Gramshree, where thousands of women were empowered through handicrafts, or one could sit outside Gandhiji's room at the Ashram listening to Sureshbhai tell stories from Gandhiji's life while the rain fell so lightly on the leaves of the strong neem trees.

~

Also from Ahmedabad came Design for Change, an idea that was born out of the Riverside School. Over time, it would put Teach For India's student vision into action through a design competition that would encourage children and Fellows to think deeply about a problem they wanted to solve together. Over the years, many Design for Change projects emerged. Sanaya's children thought up 100 ways to make people happy using the Arts. Payoshini's students developed a financial model for their parents. Adhishree's children set up 'The School of Little Designers', where her students designed solutions to social problems. Shashank's children held a fair at their school and set up stalls with games to raise the money to buy the first-ever computer in their school.

'Unlike the higher-income schools, my students didn't

have a computer. Our students felt this wasn't fair, and tried hard to raise small amounts from their community. They could only raise Rs 3000, which was not nearly enough for a computer. Our students Nisha and Huma had an idea—what if they held a fair at school to raise the money? The Sunrise English Medium School sprang into action. Over weeks, beautiful craft items like paper flowers and bags were made, and games and food stalls planned. A thousand people came to the Fun Fair, which raised Rs 13,000, enough to buy "our" computer, as my children put it.'

—Shashank Shukla, 2010 Teach For India Alumnus; Mason Fellow, Harvard Kennedy School; Chairman, Gurukul Group of Institutions

Once a year, the most innovative Design For Change projects from across the world would be invited to a 'Be The Change Conference' at the National Institute of Design (NID) in Ahmedabad. Students ran the conference, and children from India and many other countries would come together to design their future. Shireesha and her friends in Hyderabad were concerned about the weight of their hugely burdensome school bags, so they designed a project that reduced the weight of their school bags by 50 percent. In Gujarat, Ravi and his friends envisioned a tobacco-free world. They boycotted school and went on a hunger strike at home until their teacher and family members quit smoking. Ten-year-old Bindi and her friends in Rajasthan tackled the stigma around India's so-called 'untouchable' caste. They swept roads, insisting on being treated as though they were 'untouchables', and finally went on a hunger strike until the adults of their village agreed to examine the situation and correct it.

Children in Singapore developed an awareness campaign to better understand the significance of school janitors. They placed posters of the school's employees alongside stories of their lives, hoping to broaden the horizons of their community. In Taiwan, Zhang and Chen discovered that their visually impaired friend Jack was too shy to make friends, so they invited Jack to touch their faces, enabling him to 'see' who they were. Shaheen visited Chile as part of a Teach For All conference and stumbled across a project close to her own heart; Chilean children had set up a rock band to perform in a community and when people came to watch, they showed them pictures of puppies in the community that needed to be adopted.

∼

Shaheen learnt from her friend Ian Desai, a Gandhian scholar, how to better understand the contribution that Gandhian thought had to teaching. Gandhiji's belief was that the transformation of society followed from community-level transformation that in turn followed from the transformation of the individual. The classroom was the best laboratory for instigating and nurturing such individual transformation in students.

Gandhiji knew that his mission started with himself, with his ability to 'Be the Change'. Teach For India had seen that the transformation of students was greatly affected by the teachers who guided and shaped their learning experience.

Its growing focus on the personal transformation of its Fellows was an extension of this idea. Gandhiji was always aware that in order to reach his vision he would need the support and collaboration of a network of individuals. The countless contributors to his struggle for independence and social change are not acknowledged often enough. In Gandhiji's own words, 'I have shone with the glory borrowed from my innumerable co-workers.'

Gandhi believed that he could resolve conflict with love, faith, and compassion. When Teach For India Fellows encountered daily challenges, they were similarly asked to face them with faith and love, and then redouble their efforts. Gandhiji believed he could turn salt into freedom. Teach For India Fellows needed to be able to maintain this kind of fantastical faith, they needed to be able to create resources from refuse.

In his writing Gandhiji describes his life as a series of experiments. Teach For India classrooms were laboratories in which experimenting would take place; spaces where Fellows were immersed in a microcosm of social issues and challenges to solve them, one step at a time. Gandhiji believed in the balance of head, hand, and heart; he believed that process determined product. If Teach For India could only maintain a steady balance of head, hand, and heart, its impact on education could only be a direct reflection of that equity.

In 2014, there were still schools in Ahmedabad where no learning was happening, as four grade levels sat in one classroom and parents had the unstable vocation of procuring and selling illicit liquor. The hope was that Teach For India could gain access to these classrooms; that with

Gandhian values held within themselves Fellows could inspire the children to want to learn. That Teach For India could then take seeds from the Ahmedabad environment and plant them across the nation, and then the world. Saahil relocated once again leaving Hyderabad, to bring Teach For India Ahmedabad to life.

Five years earlier, Saahil had been one of the Niners who had gathered at the very place where Gandhiji conceptualized the ideals upon which India gained freedom. Teach For India's mission was, in the minds of the Niners gathered there, the second struggle for the freedom of India: freedom from the stark inequities that plagued our people. Ahmedabad had allowed them the space and opportunity to take the leap of faith, to believe that an India where all children attained an excellent education was possible.

Five years later, Teach For India had 48 Fellows *teaching* in Ahmedabad. Saahil would lead a site focused on cultivating in the Fellows the intellect of Nehru, the compassion of Mother Teresa, and the moral fibre of Gandhiji. The staff and Fellows of Teach For India would aspire to return a small part of the love and learning Ahmedabad had given to them.

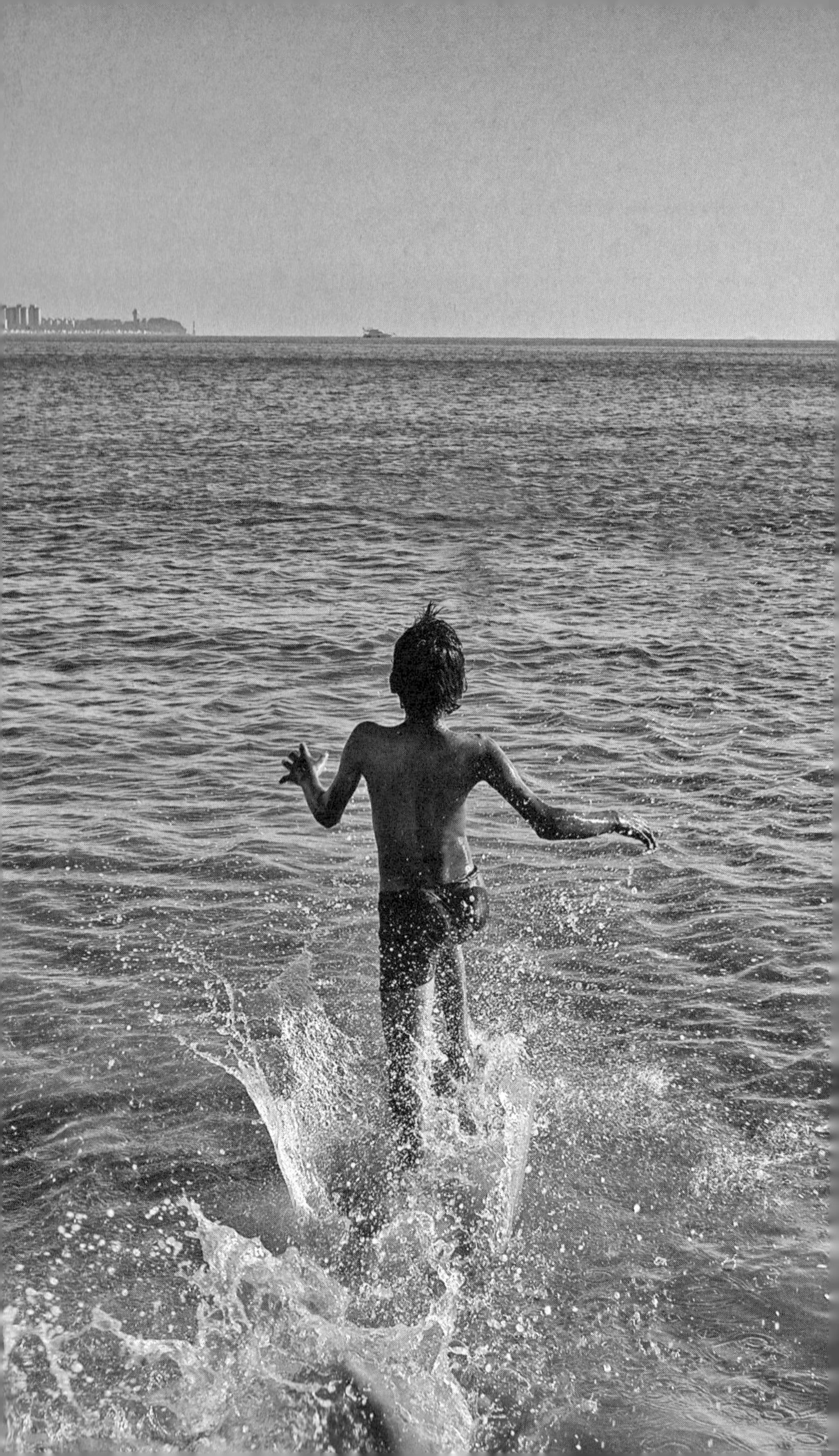

CHAPTER 11

THE PATH SO FAR

Change will come,
The path is long, and steep.
We promise kids,
The right to dream.
And promises are made to keep,
For dreams are precious things to teach.
And dreams are precious things to reach.[*]

---

[*] Shaheen's address to 2014 Fellows at Opening Ceremony

In 2014, Teach For India simplified leadership into a path of three commitments. The first was the Commitment to Personal Transformation.

'I grew up believing it was childish to cry, it was ridiculous to say I failed, and totally unacceptable to be weak in front of other people. I was told that "I" had the power to take my life in any direction and that "I" was responsible for where I was in life. Little did I know I would shatter each of these notions at the age of 22. Being around my children showed me how to live my emotions every day, every moment. They taught me to be honest and vulnerable. Being around my children also taught me that the "I" was not always the all-powerful. That there were forces at play far beyond the understanding of the 22-year-old who stepped in thinking she could change the world. It was the start of a journey of asking difficult questions and of seeing the world with all its complexities.'

—Kanika Saraff, 2009 Teach For India Alumnus and Research Lead, Reimagine Learning Community

Five years had solidified the belief that Teach For India's vision was first and foremost about inner growth, it was about who we wanted our children and ourselves to be. Personal transformation often happened when people were thrown into deep water.

> *'I was asked in my first Institute as a brand new staff member to lead the welcome session that Shaheen normally led the night before Fellows arrived. At that time, I really disliked public speaking and the thought of our brand new Fellows' first impressions being shaped by me was terrifying. After that session, people would see a changed Venil; I was raring with energy and bursting to share.'*
>
> —Venil Ali, 2009 Teach For India Alumnus and City Director, Mumbai

The Teach For India experience has been designed to cataylze personal transformation.

On 'Ownership Day' Fellows were asked to teach summer school with no staff; they had to independently navigate the challenges of their classrooms. 'Flow with Love,' another example, was a day where Fellows and staff could opt to spend 24 hours with neither money nor shelter, in an attempt to connect with the kindness of strangers. Romana and Venil remember taking up this challenge, leaving their bags and wallets behind and confronting their fears by lying down to rest on a sidewalk. At 8 pm, on that cold Ahmedabad night, a man drove past them twice, slowing down. On his third pass, he pulled over and asked them what they were doing, and said it wasn't safe. He left only to return yet again, to insist he would call their parents unless they went to sleep at the nearby temple. The man eventually locked them *inside* the temple to make sure they were safe. That evening challenged both of them to think about faith differently, while simultaneously bringing up questions about their fears and misconceptions.. But more than anything they remember how the experiences they shared on that night started an enduring friendship between them.

On an arranged visit to India, staff members from Teach For All countries across the world visited local communities in one of Teach For India's most beloved activities, the 'Yellow Hat'. Here, Fellows, staff, and participants went out into the community, playing cricket with children, or even giving a vegetable vendor time off while they manned their stall.

A group of Teach For India staff members and *Moved by Love* volunteers visited a crowded city park where they gave out 'have a nice day' cards, and simply smiled at strangers. Meghna Rakshit, the Communications Director at Teach For India, remembers feeling outside of her comfort zone until she saw one of her group members, Kanishka, approach a homeless, half-naked man carrying a huge plastic bag of garbage. 'All of a sudden, Kanishka gives this literally naked, hunched-over man a massive hug that must have lasted for twenty seconds. And this was the breaking moment for me. All this stuff I'm trying to do, it was nothing in comparison to that.'

Personal transformation at Teach For India comes from the incessant efforts of Fellows and staff to address the seemingly countless classroom and community challenges: a death in a family, an abusive neighbour, or a serious illness. Ritika, a small girl, was absent one day. Four days later, the children came to school with news that she had died. Her Fellow was left trying to understand how a parent could choose to attempt to heal their dangerously ill child with faith over medicine. It arose in seeing how parents with no means were repeatedly bearing children that they couldn't afford to raise. It arose in people asking questions, triggered by challenges and situations.

When Fellows at first objected to the idea of selecting Teach For India's most transformational classrooms as part of the Transformational Impact Journey, they were asked to reflect on questions like 'Why does one person's success have to undermine another person? What is wrong with celebrating and learning from individual excellence? What can we do to make Teach For India a place that it is safer for people to both fail and excel in?' It was not just the experience of teaching class during the Fellowship that led to personal transformation; it was the act of reflecting on that experience and using it to understand oneself a little better.

~

The Commitment to Collective Action.

Three years after he was inducted into the Alumni Movement, Sidharth got a call from one of his former student's parents. Doctors had diagnosed Sapna with leukaemia. 'For an hour, I was shattered, and then I said we just have to fix this. Four Fellows over the years had taught Sapna; we could figure this out together.' What happened afterwards represented an amazing turn of events.

Sidharth reached out to Jo Chopra, who he knew from Teach For India's TEDx years earlier, and she connected him to a woman who she knew in Mumbai. Through the generosity of this woman and through his personal network, Sidharth raised the 2.5 lakhs needed for Sapna's treatment. He discovered at Institute the following year that the donor, who had no connection to Sapna, happened to be the mother of an incoming Fellow. Sapna recovered fully; scored 92 percent on her 8th standard exams, and entered class nine.

The Commitment to Collective Action was about building relationships and organizing partnerships that would maximise Teach For India's impact. Teach For India knew that it could only be a small part in reaching the vision of *all* children receiving an excellent education; instead, people across India would need to work together—this would ultimately unleash Teach for India's unimaginable potential.

'Teach For India is a web of bonds with people, a network of relationships, an awakening of the realization of our inter-connectedness. I have come to slowly realize that each one of us is part of this web, where each one's action affects another, where each one has a role to play in contributing to this web, in making it stronger, bigger, and better.'

—Madhumita Subramanium, 2009 Teach For India Alumnus, ED.M in Mind, Brain and Education from the Harvard Graduate School of Education, and Assistant Teacher, Peabody Terrace Children's Centre

One of the things that inspired this Commitment was

'many-to-many,' a concept that came from the ruminations of Nipun Mehta, the founder of Servicespace.com and a close friend of Jayeshbhai. To Nipun, Gandhiji was a 'one to many' leader; one great leader inspiring many to follow. Vinobha Bhave, on the other hand, was a 'one-to-one' leader; one person connecting with another to inspire giving. Nipun believed that internet technology presented the opportunity to connect in a many-to-many way; the way that nature itself was all connected.

> *'In the Gandhi 3.0 version, there is a many-to-many framework at play. The person next to you is 'being the change' and you are 'being the change' and the person next to him or her is also creating his or her own ripples with transformation-driven action. This then, has the potential to create infinite possibilities in shifting our consciousness, especially with modern-day tools and technologies.'*
>
> — Nipun Mehta, Founder, ServiceSpace

In this model, the circle created a complete and significant space where anyone could speak or listen. This idea grew into Teach For India's next version of the 'open forum', which was called the 'learning circle'. The learning circle consisted of a group of Fellows and a Programme Manager who were there to inspire and support one another. Previously, Fellows' primary responsibilities included only their class of children and their own leadership development. Now, Fellows would be responsible for the over 400 children that *all* the Fellows in their learning circle taught—and they were also responsible for the development of the other Fellows in their circle. It was a daunting amount of responsibility, but it also meant each one of them received much more resilient and consistent support. Learning circles weren't exclusive for Fellows; staff members across the organization adopted the idea. Weekly meetings and retreats became spaces where teams would sit in circles and everyone would be responsible for each the group's collective support and accountability.

In practice, Collective Action proved difficult to actually achieve. Teach For India staff often shared concerns that they weren't communicating directly enough, or trusting each other's intention, or collaborating as meaningfully and often as they would like. Within the classroom, Fellows were often repeating the same mistakes as their earlier counterparts, only because they weren't listening to and learning from each other enough. However when it worked, Collective Action had a profound and an enduring impact.

Five years after Tarun and Aditya started teaching, their school was demolished overnight. Admittedly, it was housed in an unsafe, tin-roofed building, and the municipality had been threatening to demolish the structure for more than five years. When he had first arrived, Tarun had spoken at length with students' parents about the dilapidated structure and the risks it presented. When the demolition actually occurred years later, the parents organized, went to the media and had their story published; 300 students no longer had a school. The public pressure forced the school owner to rebuild the school. Tarun and Aditya's kids would not only have a safe environment in which to learn, but along with their parents and communities, would never forget the power they had when they worked together.

~

Third, was the Commitment to Educational Equity.

> 'If I were to be born again, what are the odds that I would go to University? I believe that a child's opportunity for fulfilling his or her potential must not be determined by birth. How enduring is my commitment to an equitable and just India?'
>
> —Tarun Cherukuri, 2009 Teach For India Alumnus and City Director, Delhi

This commitment was about deepening Teach For India's understanding of the complex and difficult realities that arose from educational inequity, cultivating an enduring belief that the problem was solvable, and committing to the attainment of the overarching solution, an excellent education for *all* children.

In 2014, the path to getting to educational equity still remains unclear. Teach For India started the year with a vision of 'One Day', but eventually declared that 50 years from now, all children in India would attain an excellent education. It evolved from weekly goals that were set to get the Fellowship off the ground in 2009, into five more systematic organizational goals:

1. recruit and develop Fellows
2. put students on a transformed life path
3. connect and mobilize Alumni to calayze change in education
4. generate national focus around the need for educational equity and
5. build a great, enduring institution

~

Teach For India organized the path into three 'phases'. Phase 1 (2009-13) had been the first five years, which were marked by getting Teach For India off the ground. That included establishing both the Fellowship and an Alumni movement that demonstrated multiple proof points of success, rapid growth, and cultivating a belief that 50 years was possible.

> *'In Phase 1, we asked ourselves the question "How do we start strong?" We wanted to build a credible brand and generate momentum around our vision, hire outstanding, driven people, and to think deeply about how we could put our children on a different life path and evolve a vision for our students. We knew we needed to build an effective, influential, and credible board, to define our model and adapt it to the context of each community, to secure significant funding, to create strong starting systems and processes that would enable us to grow, and perhaps most importantly, we needed to build a culture of passion and urgency that was firmly embedded in our core values.'*

In those five years, Teach For India had taught 23,000 children, placed Fellows in 200 schools, clearly defined the model, evolved a student and Fellow vision, refined how they recruited and selected, and grew from 87 Fellows to 730 Fellows. It also expanded from 8 staff members to 150, built a strong mainstream and social media presence, secured 94 crores of funding, received strong support from 6 city governments, built momentum through 9 inspirED conferences, trained over 1100 Fellows in 9 institutes, and built a strong and committed board of directors.

The second phase of Teach For India, starting in 2014, would ask the question 'How can we have the greatest possible impact?' Phase 2 would be a time of steadier growth, of greater programmatic focus on depth and a clearer vision of systemic impact.

Teach For India's thinking on the importance of Alumni leading the change had evolved significantly from Shaheen and Anand Shah's conversation outside IIM Ahmedabad in 2008 about '50 places we want our Fellows to be after they graduate from the Fellowship'. The focus was now on creating a career fair, aligning Alumni with opportunities, and piecing them together with other Alumni in places where they could best lead changes in the quality of education. Gayatri and Tomos would map out specific leadership positions that they hoped Alumni would one day hold, hypothesize on their success rate in getting there, and work backwards to determine the number of Fellows they needed to to make it happen. From 2008 to 2014, Teach For India had become far more strategic; today, each of its six cities has a clear vision document with a strategic plan that outlines initial steps to reach their goals over the next two years.

In order to drive deeper classroom and Alumni impact, Teach For India introduced the Leadership Development Journey at the 2014 Institute. It was a four-step leadership framework. The first enabled Fellows to identify where they were on a 'student vision scale' that measured progress in academic achievement, values, and mindsets, as well as exposure and access. Next the framework allowed Fellows to track their growth on the Three Commitments: Personal Transformation, Collective Action, and Educational Equity. Once they knew where they were, it detailed the 'how' of developing leadership and outlined specific competencies to develop, while providing an ecosystem of support that Fellows could access in order to grow as leaders. A modified version of the Leadership Development Journey would later be rolled out for all staff members.

In Phase Two, Teach For India would dramatically improve the facility of its internal communication and its external media presence. It would aim to develop the next level of excellence in all systems, policies, and processes, focusing especially on staffing and attrition, which continued to be areas of concern. Fund-raising would continue to be a major area of focus with a 2014 budget of 43 crores. City-level Alumni movements would begin to show the power of a collective movement. Teach For India would start identifying and supporting Alumni exemplars in prioritized pieces of the puzzle.

Most importantly, Teach For India would continue to be true to its culture and core values, and to ensure all of the people and processes that existed within Teach For India were aligned to those values. Across the organization, staff and Fellows would act according to four clearly defined aspects of their culture: Truth and Hope, The Three Commitments, Many-to-Many, and Love.

~

At the five-year benchmark, the Teach For India team decided to practice what they considered to be their most intrinsic value — self-reflection. Truth and Hope had become a way of looking at not just their work but at the world. It was the belief that one has to confront one's true self and situation, while maintaining a non-negotiable sense of possibility; that there was and would always be something that *you* could do to make *yourself* and the world better. The Yellow Hat had now become a symbol of this idea, not just in India, but across the world. In 2014, Javier Rogla, the Founder and CEO of Ensena Spain, would share the story at a Teach For All Board Meeting in London of the impact that doing the Yellow Hat activity in Mumbai had on him. In a completely foreign community, with no cultural context or even common language, he had been inspired to dance the Macarena in order to earn a few coins to feed people in the community. To Javier, if this was possible, anything was. He would go back to Spain and make yellow thread bands for everyone to wear as a reminder of the idea of possibility. At the London board meeting, he would tie these bands on the high-powered board members as they offered their wrists in commitment.

At the heart of the idea of Truth and Hope existed a mirror. When injustice and inequity presented itself, the mirror reflected and reminded one to ask the powerful question, 'What will I do about it?' Looking through the magnifying glass made challenges larger, external and therefore problems unsolvable. Choosing the mirror could make one see that the only thing one can really change is oneself. In order to end educational inequity, Teach For India had to understand the hard truth of this and then cultivate a hope bigger than the challenges the Fellows and staff encountered every day, let alone the enormity of the problem as a whole. It was facing this mirror, and reaching inward to grasp an infinite hope, that would enable Teach For India to get to 50 years.

However hope alone would not get Teach For India to its goal. There were three commitments that each person connected with Teach For India were asked to make. If every child, staff member, Fellow, and Alumni committed to the common vision of educational equity, the hard work of transforming themselves, *and* the belief that it would take all of us working together to get there, Teach For India's vision would become a reality. The power of 'and' was deeply rooted in the three commitments.

Teaching *and* Leadership.

While Fellows committed to a transformed life path for their students in the short term, they also committed to their own leadership development in order to scale their achievements into exponentially more impactful ones to benefit children in the long-term.

The Path *and* the Vision.

While Teach For India worked urgently for the outcome of a redrawn India where every person had the opportunity to meet his or her potential, the journey increasingly became the focus. Every moment of every day mattered; filling the needs of the people around you in that moment mattered. All the little things that one thought, said, and did, added up to make the biggest difference. Giving one's all really meant trying to be one's best most of the time.

During Shaheen's annual performance appraisal, Teach For India's Chief Financial Officer, Dimple, recalled that they had been together in an important meeting some months before, when Shaheen saw a little ant walk across the table. Seeing it disoriented, and worried that the ant would get squashed under someone's notebook or mug, she excused herself for a moment to take the ant out of the office.

The Forest *and* the Trees.
At Institute each year, one of the first ideas presented was that of the Forest and the Trees. Remaining big-picture, connected to the deepest why *and* thinking through last-detail execution became a way of life at Teach For India. When team members would get too lost in their individual goals, or start putting process first, they would be pulled back to the purpose of why they were there.

Me *and* We.
Everyone at Teach For India thought about colours: the colours of each person, of each child, and of the movement. Five years down the line, they knew that this was a deeply personal journey but also about the collective. The scope of what they were trying to do was too vast for them not to be the best individuals they could be *and* the best collective.

Push *and* Be Gentle.
Fellows and staff said that their greatest growth came from challenges which required to confront one's greatest fears and overcome the seemingly impossible. Throughout, Shaheen would repeat over and over, 'be gentle'. If each person did not look after his or herself, they could not sustain the long journey ahead. Fellows and staff struggled with this but began to take small steps. They would experiment with meditation, eat more healthily, spend more time with family. Check-ins with managers would include discussions on how each person was feeling and what they needed to do to take care of themselves. Reflection was constant, and feedback was given in the spirit of deep care for a person or process improving.

> *'Teach For India has a fierce commitment to reflection and improvement. Fifteen of us sat in the basement of a Delhi house, watching video after video of Teach For India Fellows and their students and then discussing in great and painful detail whether these classrooms met the bar we needed to meet in order to achieve real systemic change. I was just blown away by the level of thoughtfulness, honesty, and self-critique that the team was engaging in — all in service of doing more of what was right for the children with whom we work. It's the stuff that makes your brain hurt. But in the best way.'*

—Mariyam Farooq, Teach For America Alumnus and Senior Director, Student, and Participant Impact, Teach For All

Music *and* Silence.
From the first day when Fellows were welcomed onto the stage with the song 'I Hope You Dance' to all the many colourful songs they sang along with their children in class, music was an intrinsic part of Teach for India's world. As the organization developed over years silence began to assume an important role as well. Meetings would often start and end with two minutes of meditation, sometimes entire sessions would be held in silence, and a now formalized focus on the internal journey began to assume a greater significance.

∼

The most significant reflection over the first five years was also the simplest; every person who was a part of the Teach For India story had in some way been the recipient of a gift of love, and that this gift rippled and would continuously transform those people and communities that it touched.

The children radiated love for their Fellows and the Teach for India staff. There was no other job in the world where you entered your office and were flooded by watermelon-sized smiles and 'Hi Didi, how are you Bhaiya?' and where birthdays made you feel like a rockstar with a slew of letters and cards, sometimes replete with a drooping rose, one that had been kept in the shade and carefully carried all day.

Mridvika Mathur, Teach For India's Development Director, volunteered in a classroom in Mumbai and gave little Aseem her phone number when he asked for it. Months later, he called and asked her to come in to his class the following day. Mridvika said yes and made a mental note, but she had two important meetings and was not sure she could make it. He texted her again that night, and yet again in the morning asking her again to please come that day, as it was his Nandita Didi's birthday. Moved by his persistence, Mridvika cancelled her meetings, bought a cake, and went in to Aseem's class. He was beaming as she walked in and said he *knew* she would come. 'How did you know I would come?' she asked. Aseem said, 'I read in your eyes when I met you that when you make a commitment, you will come.'

Love was the greatest gift that the children of Teach For India received in return from the fellows. Karthik Rapaka remembers meeting his student Sohail on his first day of school because the first thing he asked him was, 'Bhaiya, how will you hit me? With a stick, with a ruler, making me walk like a chicken, or sitting out in the sun?' Karthik was shocked. 'I am not going to hit you,' he said. It took Sohail months to believe that, but Karthik gently cared for and believed in him, and Sohail would pat his grade level in two years, and become a speaker at Hyderabad's first inspirED conference. Sohail's school Principal was in the audience. She had seen him progress from not knowing his alphabet to a 3rd grade level reading level in less than two years.

Teach For India Fellows gave their classrooms inspirational names, put up photographs of each child, celebrated birthdays, hugged their students tight, listened intently to them when they spoke of problems at home, visited their student's families regularly, and raised the money needed to give the kids magical experiences outside of class. They showed their love by holding high the bar of success, and by pushing their children to stretch. Shy children now spoke confidently in front of the whole class. Children who had struggled with a subject now loved it. Children who were scared of a difficult conversation with a parent, now bravely initiated those conversations. The Fellows and staff, the children and their parents, all felt grateful for every hard won success.

Arnab Datta spent 19 hours with his student Sakshi, who lives on the sidewalk outside Metro Cinema as her family doesn't have a home. Three things struck him as he sat on their piece of the sidewalk.

'The first was the way Sakshi's mother cooked. They had taken scrap plywood from around the area, and she broke it down with a brick, threw it into a fire, and cooked using that. I had yet to see cooking without some kind of gas fuel, but they were just using wood to heat and cook their food. The second was how a water tanker that leaked out the back was their running water. They wash their hands, and sometimes bathe in the leaking water from that water tanker. The last was that before we went to sleep, Sakshi's mother put small pieces of cloth into each child's ears, and when I inquired why, she said it was to keep bugs from crawling in.

"These things might seem inconsequential, but to me they really stuck out as signs of just how different their lives were from mine. Maybe to some extent you can understand what it feels like to be able to buy less, or see others with more. But having to do little things like put cloth in your child's ears to keep insects from crawling in when they sleep, these are the little things that are a daily part of life for families like Sakshi's, things that I could never really fathom or at least not ever fully understand.

I am lucky. After I woke up, I went to school, and then at the end of the day, I got to go home and eventually sleep in a comfortable, warm bed. Sakshi had lived on that sidewalk all the five years of her life. I feel very lucky to have grown up and lived the life I have. I hope that Sakshi can one day feel that lucky too.'

—Arnab Datta, 2010 Teach For India Fellow and former Teacher, 3.2.1 schools

The five years that Teach for India had existed were filled with small acts of kindness that rippled out and added up to a simple and profound lesson for all those who were touched by the organization; the world could change through love. With this, Teach For India had the daunting task ahead to envision Phase 3, in which Teach For India would determine a model for depth and scale with a clearer line to the realization of their vision, an excellent education for all children.

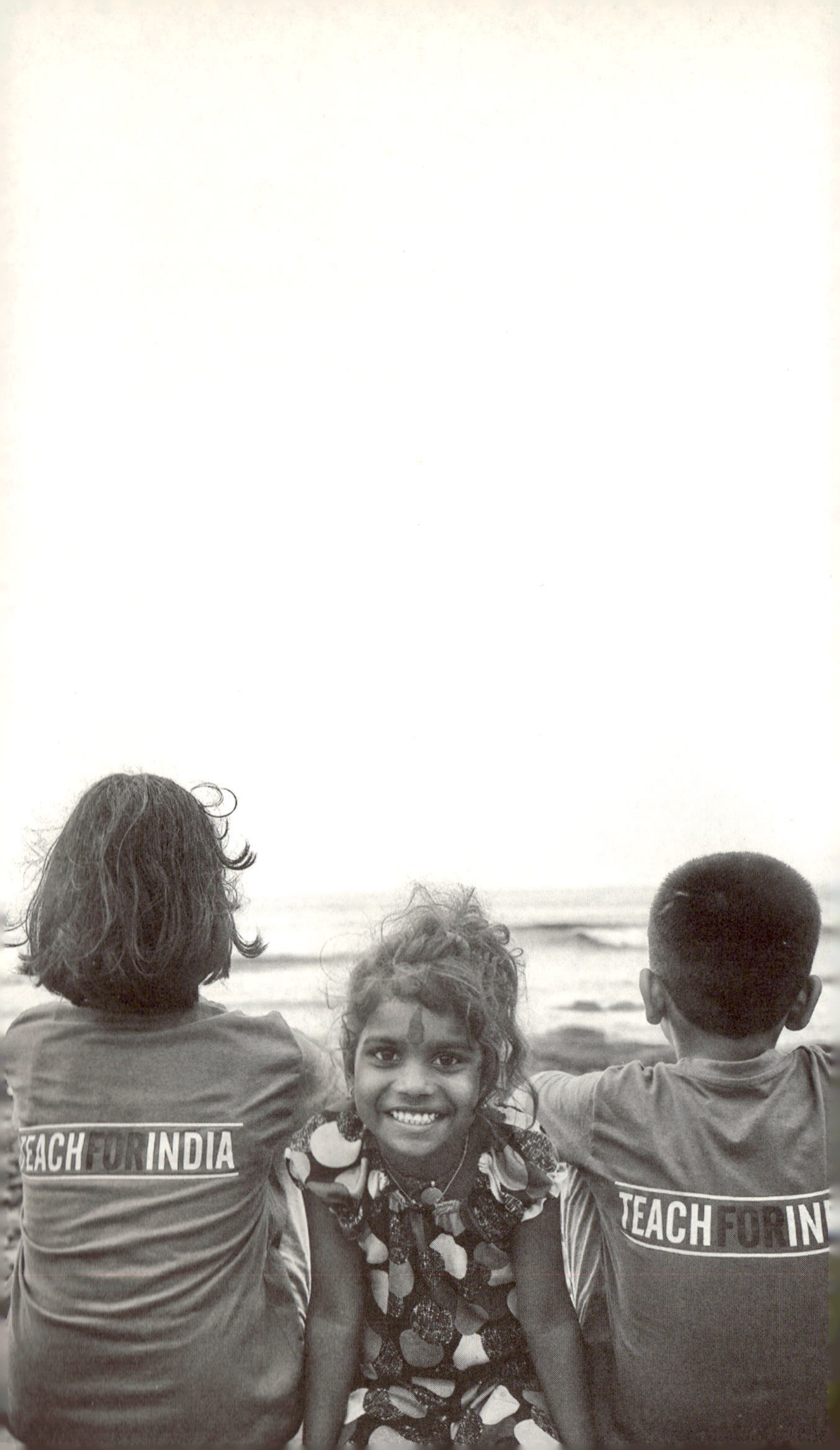
TEACH FOR INDIA
TEACH FOR IN

CHAPTER 12

FIND YOUR LIGHT

'Your light will shine as bright as any star,
For when you find your voice,
You'll find out who you are.'*

---

* Line from the Maya Musical song 'Find Your Voice' lyrics by David Goldsmith, music by Georgia Stitt

I often think about what I believe 50 years from now will look like. I want to believe that it will be so different than what I could ever know, beyond even my imagination. There are those times when I have been my best self, or seen others at their best, that have felt so gloriously and undeniably right. A world where everyone has the opportunity to be his or her best seems radical, and at the same time, unimaginably beautiful.

A year and a half ago, I had the opportunity to go back and do what I did when I was eighteen, to teach again. I wanted to know and love a group of children again. I wanted to give them everything I had learnt about education. I wanted to see our student vision in action myself so I could believe that academics, values, and exposure could be seamlessly integrated and drive fundamental change. I would work with a group of children on a musical that I had written called Maya. The Maya musical was a fantastical tale of a princess looking for her light; the story of every single child in search of their potential.

For the next eighteen months, I used any spare moment I could to support the Maya children and their main teacher directors, Sanaya Bharucha and Nick Dalton. Sanaya had taken all she had learnt in the Fellowship to a new level of excellence, establishing even closer bonds with her children and their families and providing them a space where they felt both secure and challenged within the framework of the class. Nick is an actor and dancer who relocated from Broadway to pull off what would grow into a larger-than-life symbol of what was possible for all children. Loving and energized, he would animate the kids in his rehearsals, expecting a level of professionalism that, when reached, would serve as proof points for the children themselves of their own real artistic ability. My younger daughter, Sana, joined the Maya class as well. She would spend two summers with her new friends and anxiously wait for the weekends we could travel to Pune for a class that built her confidence, and encouraged her to dance. Maya was rife with the most heart-warming, difficult, and life-changing experiences. We wanted our children to learn many of the most important lessons that many of us had only learnt as adults: how to focus, look inward, be kind, confess, and make themselves vulnerable. Class would start and end with a powerful sharing circle where we meditated together, reflected on the values we had and hadn't demonstrated that week, and shared deeply from the experience of our lives. These circles would make Maya feel like a second family for our children, and for Sanaya, Nick, and me.

Maya classes were always true to our student vision, and the need to integrate academics, values, and exposure. When we learnt to read music, we learnt fractions. When we rehearsed the song 'Hey monkey!' we watched videos to first learn and then write about the characteristics of monkeys. We exposed the children to different traditions in dance. The Maya children travelled together, sharing with Fellows and staff what they were learning and how their thinking was evolving. The group lived at the Institute with our Fellows, mirroring the intensity of the Fellow training calendar with their own packed schedule of dance, drama, language, music, and values lessons. Each day ended with a written reflection.

2014 was filled with Maya stories.

Ever-smiling Yash shared his passion for cooking with us, bringing the hot pav-bhaji that he had made for all of us to class. Priyanka received a rose from a boy through another boy, and gave it back to him with a smile, telling him his 'sister' sent it back, with love. There was the day that all the children were told that they'd be in a swimming pool the next morning, and that night had to find the courage they'd need to submerge themselves in water for the first time in their lives.

Amadeo di Lodovico, a Director at McKinsey, and Fabiana his wife, who had worked with Akanksha years earlier, brought their three children from Dubai to spend the day with the Maya kids. The children had decided to make a 'gratitude tree' and cut out coloured paper shapes. They carried their tree with the hanging paper shapes to the sea-face, and started talking to people on their evening stroll about what it was exactly that gratitude meant to them. People's reactions varied from scoffing at the children to giving them a hug as the children requested that each person take just a minute to write down something that they were grateful for and hang it on their tree. The children performed songs and danced at the sea-face, and an elderly couple who were watching from a bench called me over. Some of our Maya girls had started talking to them, and had given them big hugs. 'Today is our Anniversary,' they said, 'and in all these years we've never received so much love.' They asked if we had time to bring all our thirty children to their home for dinner. At the end of that day, we sat in our sharing circle, talking about the values we lived and didn't live through that day. As Amadeo left, he told me that he'd bring his family back to India for the Maya performance later that year, and said to me, 'Don't ever let anyone tell you otherwise. Teach For India Fellows are changing the world for their kids.'

We began to see staggering results. Academically, after a year of working with them, the Maya children were all performing above average in their regular classrooms, and on average had made almost twice as much growth as other Teach For India students. Their language fluency and choice of vocabulary was dramatically higher than it had been. They were self-aware, thoughtful about the values they wanted to live, and deliberate in practicing actions aligned to those values. The next step was to incorporate what had worked with the Maya children across Teach For India and beyond.

In a class that Teach for India held jointly with the heads of training and programme from Teach For All partners across the world, the Maya children and Teach For All partner staff explored what the student vision meant to them; what it meant to 'Find your light'. At the end of the class, the Maya children sang 'This little light of mine', and ran to spontaneously say goodbye to each person in attendance. That night, Noor, one of the staff members from Teach For Qatar, couldn't sleep. She remembered crying at the end of class as little Chaitrali hugged her and said, 'Didi, don't worry. You will find your light.' Noor, whose name translates to 'light', wrote a poem that night.

'I am grateful for my name,
The one I once hated.
But more so for the ones that taught me what it meant.
"Didi, find your inner light and shine. Dare to share and find courage."
I am grateful for this moment,
Sitting on the side of this street.
Facing mountains where a light,
So bright shines facing me.
Questioning where it was that I,
Lost my light, smiling that they helped me find it.
I am grateful that I remembered,
How magical they are.
The embodiment of light on this earth,
The reason for everything,
And the reason for all that we do...'

—Noor Al Khater, Head of Training and Support,
Teach For Qatar

The Maya story was a journey of wisdom, courage, and compassion and was inspired by Gandhiji's idea of head, hand, and heart. It captured Teach For India's greatest learning in the three questions that Maya had to face and answer as the story reaches its climax. What are the biggest things in life? What are you willing to be? What are you willing to give? Maya would answer that the biggest things were the little things, that she was willing to be the change, and that she was willing to give her *all* for that which she believed in.

Maya gave words to an idea that I had believed in from

the time I first started my work at 18. These were 'find your light'. It had always been obvious to me that the purpose of my life was to find my light, and to do what I could to create the opportunities for others to discover theirs. Akanksha and Teach For India had now become contributors to an ecosystem of small and wonderful kindnesses, little miracles, and discoveries of light.

~

I wish you could have been there with me through every single account of change that I have seen happened over these five years. I know if you could you would believe in what I believe, and would find the greatest role that you could play in getting India to 50 years. You could meet Chaitrali, who lost her father and then just over a year ago, lost her mother to complications arising from a leg infection. Arhan, her former Fellow, remembers hearing the news while at Harvard, and picking up the phone nervously, unsure about what to say to a 12-year-old who now has no family. Chaitrali's voice was sparkly and animated. 'Bhaiya how are you doing?' she asked, 'How is your college?' Arhan felt he had been punched in the stomach. Through her grief she was so happy to hear from him, *she* cared about how *he* was.

I wish you could see the magic that we now know an excellent education can be, and then you would believe as I believe.

'Education is so much more than having the ability to calculate 14.9 x 17.37 to the 3rd place of decimal.

Indeed, it does involve knowing that 14.9 x 17.37 = 258.813. More importantly, however, it is about knowing that mathematical models enable us to represent the universe and all its occurrences, all its constants and idiosyncrasies, beauty and tragedy in the language of numbers, and thereby observe, record, and learn from, indeed experience the world around and beyond us in a deeper and more meaningful way.

'Yes, it is about knowing that Mississippi has 4 s's and 4 i's. But it also about understanding the inherent beauty of words; about how they make our world more lucid and yet more colourful. It is about how emotions can be expressed through them and how minds can be understood by understanding them. It is about how thoughts and ideas can be conveyed using them and how immortality can be achieved via them. Yes, it is about knowing that 'honesty is the best policy' but also understanding why this old proverb was coined; how it is not only the moral but also the most logical policy. For how with each honest hand that we deal we increase the probability of ourselves being dealt with an honest one.'

—Gaurav Singh, 2009 Teach For India Alumnus and Founder, 3.2.1 Schools

Nowadays there is much joy at Akanksha where for the last two years 100 percent, *every single child*, passed the 10th standard school-leaving exam. While we remain aware that each child has a long path ahead that is fraught with hardship and a persisting inequity, every milestone we cross increases the number of his or her opportunities exponentially. An Alumnus of the class of 2010, Seema is now the newly appointed school Principal of 3.2.1. Sameena, who I first taught when she was three, is doing her Bachelors in Special Education. When I asked Naval about her dreams for her 8-year-old daughter Mahek, who is in an Akanksha school. 'I will help her do whatever she wants to do in her life,' she says, exactly what my mother used to say, and does to this day.

Every single staff member at Akanksha has an inspiring story, and I wish you could meet them all. Joyce Christy's daughter Rachel is physically and mentally challenged. Joyce considers her daughter as a most precious blessing and decided that to give back to the world she wanted to work as a trauma counselor. Priya Agarwal and Lopa Gandhi have started Antarang, an organization that works with the most marginalized adolescents. Archana Chandra works with mentally challenged children and adults in a space called Jai Vakeel. I wish you could have been there to feel the energy when 180 Teach For India children came together to create a Model United Nations, debating climate-change, or the Indo-Pakistan border issue, or how gender disparity cripples the world.

> 'Syyed Famida Zakhir Hussain comes from a broken home, and I see the fire in her eyes every time she talks about the India-China border issue and how it can only be solved through relentless peace talks. Mohini Sagar volunteers to switch off the lights every day after school, because she believes that leaving them on will contribute to global warming; and the only time I heard Shaheen Siddqui raise her voice was during the United Nations

Human Rights council when she had to defend the rights of refugee women in the Democratic Republic of Congo. She wants to join the UN one day, to help refugee women across the world.'

—Adithya Narayanan, 2012 Teach For India Alumnus and Alumni Impact Manager, Teach For India

We hold the firm belief that one day Institute will welcome some of our students as Teach For India Fellows, that our children will be the leaders of our movement.

∼

The truth is that when we look across India and the world, these stories are the exception. The truth is that for every inspiring story there are more than equally gut-wrenching ones. While we treat our girls equally in class, we see families of four walking all with slippers except the daughter. While little Sapna pulled through Leukaemia, we lost little Vikas, Sumona, and Ritika to illnesses, which could have been survived had they been treated more effectively. While Preethi now thrives at the boarding school that Vipul integrated her into, far too many children never even start school, or if they do, drop out way too early. When you walk around in the community where I first met Pinky and started my work, you realize that just too many children are on the wrong life path, one that will never lead them to realize their potential.

Pick up the newspaper and read the headlines to remember the truth. 1.4 million Indian children aged

6-11 out of school: Unesco (the *Times of India*, July 2014)[1]. Gujarat's class 8 literates can't read, finds ASER 2012 (*DNA*, January 2013)[2]. 66% Class 8 students in Maharashtra can't subtract and divide, finds ASER (*DNA*, January 2014)[3]. January 2012: Indian students rank 2nd last in global PISA test (the *Times of India*)[4]. August 2012: India drops out of PISA. RTE unable to stem learning rot amongst tots (*Deccan Herald*, January 2013)[5]. India's landmark education law is shutting down schools (*BBC World News*, July 2014)[6]. 54 school headmasters suspended in Bihar for misusing SSA funds (*Zee News*, June 2014)[7]. Up to 20,000 teachers in Bihar hired on forged degrees (*Indian Express*, July 2014)[8]. 99% fail test for school teachers (the *Times of India*, January 2013)[9]. Aspirations bring girls to schools, lack of toilets drives them away (Livemint.com, June 2014)[10]. Banning sex education is not a solution (the *Times of India*, July 2014)[11]. 30% girls in Maharashtra are child brides (the *Times of India*, July 2014)[12]. More children are going to school in India, but they're learning less (*Time Magazine*, July 2014)[13].

There have been many efforts before the inception of Teach For India to promote higher educational standards for India's children. The mid-day meal was launched in 1995 as a way to enhance enrolment, retention, and attendance while improving the nutritional levels of students in school. The Sarva Shiksha Abhiyan, known as the Government of India's flagship programme for the achievement of the universalization of Elementary Education, has been operational since 2000. In 2009, education became a fundamental right for all children aged 6-14 through the Right to Education Act. The truth is that despite the spate of government and non-profit efforts over many years, we are still facing a deplorable state of education in our country.

~

Thirteen years ago, I remember sitting down to contemplate where Akanksha was headed. Akanksha was almost ten years old and we were impacting about 1500 children at that time. I wrote a vision, and called it 10,000 smiles. I wondered if and when we'd reach that number. Today, Teach For India reaches 30,000 children through our Fellowship alone, and countless others through the extended impact that is driven by our Alumni. When I think of the individual students, the Khalils and Akbars, Prachis and Surajs, Vijays and Mrunalis, I see the heartening significance of that number. When I think of the 200 million children of school-going age in India who are still in desperate need of an excellent education, I see the real significance in *that* number.

We are not yet sure of how to go from where we are now to catalyzing the movement for *all* children. However, we now understand the core concepts that define an excellent education. We know that Teach For India is a powerful supplier of transformational leaders across the country, and we are sure that if our collective intention is to do right by every child, then reaching our vision is inevitable. Even if we can't draw that clear line to 50 years yet, even if the path curves and sometimes goes a little black or backwards, we know at our core that we will somehow reach our destination.

Teach For India Alumni will lead the way there. They will catalyze change through their level of commitment to the belief that change *must* happen. They will inspire action through their actions. Archana and Nirali's Teacher Training Portal www.firki.co is an open-source platform for every teacher to access and improve their teaching practice. Pushkar is leading a school of 1200 students in rural Uttar Pradesh. Sriram, Anushka, Zoya, and Saurabh are school leaders in Akanksha schools. Gaurav's 3.2.1 school welcomed 360 children this year, and is now starting a teacher training wing for other teachers to learn from its practices. Ashmita teaches special needs students at the Gateway school. Sathyanand works to build a love for reading through the Karadi tales. Shrutika and Ritika train school leaders at the India School Leadership Institute. Amit and Shivani work with Dalberg Consulting, and are working on Teach For India's crowd-sourcing site. Subhashini works with McKinsey's education practice. Danny brings leaders from around the world to Teach For India through Leader's Quest. Sana just graduated from Columbia University, interned with the New York City Department on teacher education, and is exploring innovative technology and education. Arnab leaves four years of teaching to explore policy-level change through a Masters of Science in Foreign Service at Georgetown University. Aravind and Bikrama are at the Central Square Foundation, evaluating and supporting education entrepreneurs. Anushree spent time after the Fellowship understanding what it will take to drive change in Kashmir. Ajita teaches at the Azim Premji University. Fiona and Namrata work with mentoring start-ups. Meghana's Bharatiya Jain Sanghatna works on school evaluation in 104 schools across five States. Vaibhav's work with the Learning Links foundation is focused on evaluating how continuous comprehensive evaluation is working across 1000 schools. Abhik helped start up Teach For Bangladesh. Lewitt's start-up Life Labs animates science classrooms across government and low-income schools in Pune. Puneet, Iffat, Nikhat and a multitude of others continue to plan for their students every weekend and evening, and wake up to teach every weekday morning.

~

When I first met Rahul Gupta I remember thinking that he would make a great politician; I was struck by his ability to communicate his passion, and his conviction. Rahul taught in an Akanksha school in Mumbai, and then was transferred to a school in Pune that was really struggling. The school was in a desperately bad state, dilapidated with a teaching staff rampant that had lost faith, bad student behavior, a dark go-down full of broken furniture and with leaking ceilings. Visiting, I was admittedly a bit nervous and wondered where he would start. Rahul must have noticed and pulled me aside with a calm smile, 'Don't you worry. That's why *I'm* here.'

I went back to the school a year later and it felt like a different world. In Rahul's office four big goals were posted up on the board—Bridging the Achievement Gap for All Students, Parent Engagement, Teacher Development, and School Culture—and there was evidence of progress toward these goals everywhere in the school. Every single child was seated in class, engaged and studying. The school now had double the space, hard-won from the government, and had a bright and colourful new computer lab and a cheerful library. Rahul chatted with me about the eleven new programmes the team had introduced that year, including a choice of six sports for every child in secondary school, a new reading programme, a science Lab and a Teacher Leadership programme that gave his more senior teachers leadership responsibility in the school. A parent engagement programme was also in place and parents came in to set goals with their children. It was the most apparent turnaround of a school that I've ever seen, and I left just completely inspired.

> 'In our performance appraisals at the end of the year, I decided not to give any developmental feedback. I had never seen a team that had worked so hard all year. People who had struggled with things were now coaching others. It was amazing. I thought each person needed to celebrate, and so we focused on their feelings and what had made them happy.'
>
> —Rahul Gupta, 2009 Teach For India Alumnus and School Leader, Savitribhai Phule English Medium School

Trips to Teach For India schools and communities impacted the global network as well. Clarissa Delgado, the CEO of Teach For the Philippines, would say that three days immersed in Teach For India schools and communities left her with answers, more questions, and 'dogged determination, convinced that starting Teach For the Philippines was not only doable, but relevant and urgent'.

'In my first month of working at Teach For All, I met a Teach For India Fellow who earnestly believed that he could transform India within 50 years. My instinct was, to my shame, to laugh: I'd never seen such hope and sense of possibility paired with capable leadership before, and I didn't know how to respond. Within seconds, though, my laughter turned to wonder and then excitement. YES. These are the leaders we need all over the world in order to repair injustice, model love and compassion, and achieve things no one thought possible. They are the right teachers for our students, the right leaders for our countries, and the right people to love as neighbours.'

—Jen Brenneman, Senior Director, Leadership,
Teach For All

The Teach For India staff Alumni would go on to find their piece in the puzzle locally, and in the global Teach For All network. Shveta would start Talerang, an enterprise focused on preparing young people for careers. Kavita would work to support social entrepreneurs at Villagro. Chaitali would run operations at Aangan, an organization working with some of India's most marginalized children. Tomos would lead over 500 participants in Teach First's London site. Maureen and Sheela would return to Teach For America, focusing on training and leadership. Jeet Patel would join Teach For All, leading the recruitment effort for South Asia.

Over the five years, 104 Teach For India Fellows would join staff positions, committing to build Teach For India, one step at a time. Kiwa would state plainly that this was what she was born to do, and talk about her ten-year plan with

Teach For India. Sachin felt this was the place he needed to be; he believed that if there was such a thing as real change that it would come from here. Sidharth would ask,

'Why isn't there urgency around educational inequity? We feel urgency around rape, around corruption, but at the root of all of this is education. The truth is that this is a real crisis. The hope is that it's solvable. 1500 people have already walked this path. We don't know the answers, but the urgency is there to keep moving forward.'

Gaps in the puzzle of educational inequity were starting to be filled in with Teach For India Fellow and staff Alumni. They were stepping into diverse sectors—both in and out of education—and wherever they were, they were staying connected to the idea and acting to better the lives of children.

These gains were always thrilling but still were not nearly enough. Our Alumni needed resilience to stay the course, to keep sight of the destination, the dream of educational equity for *all* children. They would need to be an army, inspiring every person across India to play their necessary part in the mission. They would need to continue the journey they had all now embarked upon, inward, to search for their own light, to live the greatest lives that they could live.

∼

They say one should not have favourite children, but sometimes I do, and Latif was one of mine. I still think about him daily, how every time he walked into my classroom, he just made it better; warmer, happier, and more special. Latif was one of those kindest kinds of people. He was a beautiful child, with aspirations that lay beyond any limitations that fate saw fit to put before him. Like so many kids his age, he wanted to be a Bollywood star, but there was something about his openness, his ease, which made so many of us really believe that it may one day come to be. As the star of the 100 member cast in Akanksha's 'Kabir and the Rangeen Kurta', he held audiences riveted, hope held in their throats as they filed out of the theatre, believing with their whole hearts in the unimaginable potential of every single child in India.

About a year after the production of the Akanksha musical I was driving in my car approaching Pune when I received a call from Nikki, Latif's teacher at the time. She said he was deathly ill, and had been admitted to intensive care at a government hospital. I immediately turned my car around and drove back to Mumbai, but by the time I reached the hospital, he had passed away.

The next day, I sat next to Latif's grief-stricken grandfather who told me that concerned at the weak state of his grandson, he had taken his life savings and told him to go straightaway to see the doctor at the private hospital. Latif instead had waited until his grandfather was sleeping, and then secretly slipped the money back into his grandfather's trunk. Latif's real dream had always for his elderly grandfather to be able to retire. Six months before, with just enough money, his grandfather had finally been able to stop working. Latif had chosen to bear his sickness, severe to the point of being fatal, rather than jeopardize his grandfather's security. I remember clearly Latif's grandfather saying softly, 'I was always more important to him than he was to himself.'

I do not know if Latif would have survived had he received better medical care. What I do know is that day changed my perspective forever. I always knew every human being had so much potential to give, but what Latif taught me was that the human capacity to give, and to love, is beyond life itself, and is limitless.

The Maya script had been completed before Latif died. Maya was perhaps my way of keeping his memory alive, of remembering his potential. It was my way of waking up each day to the challenge of taking one more step towards my own light. A welcome reminder that all children *are* Maya, that all of them have a brilliant light inside. A reminder that with the power of this light no dream was beyond being realized, no distance existed that could not be reached, and run through.

Only opportunity separates those children who are able to find their light from those who are not, and only driven and dedicated people can provide these opportunities. Only you and I facing our inward mirrors can ask the question 'What is the greatest life I can lead?' and only you an I can take one step at a time toward living it. If we do this, then, in 50 years India will be redrawn.

AFTERWORD

Join the Movement

Over Teach For India's five-year journey, people from everywhere have contributed in their own way. We've tried to list some of these out as inspiration for you. Here are 100 ways to **Join the Movement**; small and big steps that will help us get to that day where, as 14-year-old Priyanka writes at the start of this book, 'One Day is here'.

Help find future Teach For India Fellows
- Visit the Teach For India website (www.teachforindia.org) and apply to the Teach For India Fellowship
- Join Teach For India's Facebook page. Follow Teach For India on Twitter
- Refer interested applicants to the website
- Write an article about Teach For India and/or others working in education
- Invite the Teach For India recruitment team to make a presentation at your college/company

- Encourage your company to give 2-4 paid sabbaticals to employees who want to do the Teach For India Fellowship

Connect with a Child
- Look into a child's eyes and smile, *every day*, if possible
- Create art with a child—paint, draw, make puppets, *like the Akanksha Art children!*
- Paint a mural in a school or an outdoor city wall with a group of children
- Spend a day with a child involved in labour (washing dishes, lifting loads, selling chai), *like Fellows try to in Ahmedabad*. Go for a walk with a child and ask what their dreams are
- Give a child an experience they've *never* had
- Plant trees with kids
- Play football or cricket with kids on the street, *or organize a league!*
- Gift a child a new set of clothes
- Take a sick child to a doctor you know
- Take a few street children to a movie *and see their joy!*
- Ask a child's name when you see him or her on the street
- Give a child a warm hug and a cold ice-cream!
- Spend a night in the community, *like the Teach For India Fellows do at the Institute*
- Smile and chat with children at the signal when your car stops at a red light. *Give a child a ride!*
- Cook a meal and share it with a family on the street and/or take a child out to *your* favourite restaurant *and see what a big deal it is*
- Take a child to a toy store and let them *choose* what they'd

like to buy
- Visit a slum community and talk to the people there. *Wear your Yellow Hat!*
- Organize a 'Connect with a Child' day as part of CSR at your company and have everyone teach in a school for a day. *Practice Commitment to Collective Action!*
- Visit an orphanage and play games with the kids. *Give away something, like Priyanka gave away her teddy Nia.*
- Find shelter for a homeless child. Be a big Brother/Big Sister to a child in an orphanage
- Take a child to a fun-fair, play, or concert with your family
- Conduct free health check-ups for kids if you are a doctor
- Buy a child a balloon, *or a Firki!*

Educate a Child
- Take a three month sabbatical from work and teach full-time
- Gift a book to a child and read children stories and poems
- Run a summer camp for children
- Invite your grandparents and other elderly people in to class to share stories from their life
- Read and explain your favourite poem to a child. *Try Shel Silverstein's Colors.*
- Tutor a child/family member of a person who works for you
- Grow a garden with a group of children in a municipal school
- Ask your child to give back presents at their birthday party with notes to give them away to less privileged children this year
- Start a children's choir and sing door to door

- Volunteer once a week in a Teach For India/other classroom, *and find volunteers*
- Mentor an adolescent through Akanksha's Mentoring Programme (www.akanksha.org)
- Share your passion with a group of children (writing, dance, yoga, meditation, music etc.) *Teach a child Teach For India's favourite song, 'I hope you Dance', by Lee Ann Womack*
- Ask 'what do you love doing' instead of 'what do you want to become' to children
- Start tutoring kids at a construction site
- Do a Design For Change (www.dfcworld.com) project with kids.
- Volunteer in a classroom on Children's day and do something special for the children
- Design activity-based learning aids for kids
- Conduct a student/teacher exchange between a high-income school and a low-income school
- Clean a school with a group of friends one weekend and conduct a session around sanitation in a school
- Facilitate career awareness sessions for adolescents
- Talk to children about Gandhiji and other leaders
- Coach or mentor a child's teacher, Fellow, Teach For India staff member or Alumnus

Raise Resources
- Paint an old recycled bottle, add a few coins to it every day, and when it is full do a good deed for a child with the money
- Gift board games or educational aids to a classroom. *Gift a mini-library to a classroom*

- Donate a camera to a classroom, *so children like Sapna's kids can take photos!*
- Collect your pocket money and donate it, *like the three Bharucha sisters did*
- Ask a Fellow/teacher what they need for their classroom and get that for them. *Fund a Fellow's Be The Change project*
- Support a Teach For India Alumnus' organization
- Pay a child's school or college fees. *Donate to the Ra Foundation (www.rafoundation.in) to sponsor a child in need's school fees to a top boarding school*
- Go onto the Teach For India website (www.teachforindia.org) to sponsor a Teach For India Fellow or School. *There are 930 Fellows to Sponsor!*
- Pay for a Counselor in a school, or a teacher for children with Special Needs. *Most municipal schools don't have one.*
- Donate to redecorate a government school staff room and paint a classroom
- Donate blankets, clothes, umbrellas, etc. to kids who are homeless
- Donate time in an area of skill that you have (strategy, legal expertise, journalism, anything!)
- Request people not to give you gifts on a special occasion and donate the money to Teach For India/other organizations in education instead
- Pay for a field trip for a class of children and their teachers
- Donate to build/fix a toilet in a municipal school, *so no child uses a toilet like the one in Arhan's school*
- Donate space that you have for Teach For India/other NGO training sessions, offices

- Donate a projector and/or laptops or tablets to schools
- Encourage your company to use the 2% CSR spend mandated in the Companies Act to donate to education
- Buy a plane ticket for a child who has never been on a plane, *like Nimo did for Priyanka*
- Get your company to donate towards the costs of bringing Teach For India to your city
- Clean a school or community toilet, *thinking of Jayesh Bhai*
- Donate 5 percent of your salary each month to education

Advocate for Educational Equity
- Get 10 people to visit the Teach For India website (www.teachforindia.org)
- Share the Truth and Hope campaign with 10 people http://connect.teachforindia.org/truth-hope
- Start an organization focused on education. *Start a school, like Surya did!*
- Attend an inspirED conference (www.inspiredindia.in)
- Write an op-ed on education
- Integrate out of school children into school
- Spend time educating children around your home on their basic rights
- Join Teach For India staff
- Lobby a politician to focus on primary education and make improving the quality of primary education part of the mandate in the next election
- Make sure every school has a School Management Committee. *Screen the film Taare Zameen Par for parents*
- Launch a social media campaign around education equity

- Read the ASER report and the Right To Education Act to understand the State of Education
- Visit a school on your travels
- Report a child in distress through Childline's 1098 hotline

Show Gratitude and Love
- Thank someone who has been a teacher to you
- Gift a teacher you don't know something on Teacher's Day
- Watch and share Nimo's 'Being Kind' and 'Grateful' music videos on Youtube
- Say thank you to children
- Make a seriously ill child's wish come true (www.makeawishindia.org)
- Invite Fellows and their students home or workplace for a meal
- Give a child a gift on his/her birthday
- Tell a child that he/she is important, and that he/she is loved
- Write a story about a child and gift it to them
- Be a good role-model for children
- Write notes and letters to children you love and are grateful for. *Read the story of Shel Silverstein's Giving Tree to someone and then thank your giving tree like our Fellows do*
- Keep a gratitude/reflection journal where you take two minutes before you sleep each day to write down what you are grateful for
- Find the child in you

REFERENCES

Chapter 12

1. '1.4 million Indian children aged 6-11 out of school: Unesco', *Times of India*, 7 July 2014. http://timesofindia.indiatimes.com/india/1-4-million-Indian-children-aged-6-11-out-of-school-Unesco/articleshow/37929697.cms (Accessed 9 July 2014)
2. 'Gujarat's class 8 literates can't read, finds ASER 2012', *DNA*, 19 Jan 2013. http://www.dnaindia.com/india/report-gujarat-s-class-8-literates-can-t-read-finds-aser-2012-1790374 (Accessed 9 July 2014)
3. '66% Class 8 students in Maharashtra can't subtract and divide, finds ASER', *DNA*, 16 Jan 2014. http://www.dnaindia.com/academy/report-66-class-8-students-in-maharashtra-cant-subtract-and-divide-finds-aser-1951598 (Accessed 9 July 2014)
4. 'Indian students rank 2nd last in global PISA test', *Times of India*, 15 Jan 2012. http://timesofindia.indiatimes.

com/home/education/news/Indian-students-rank-2nd-last-in-global-test/articleshow/11492508.cms (Accessed 8 July 2014)
5. 'India drops out of PISA. RTE unable to stem learning rot amongst tots', *Deccan Herald*, 17 Jan 2013. http://www.deccanherald.com/content/306095/rte-unable-stem-learning-rot.html (Accessed 10 July 2014)
6. Francis, Alys. 'India's landmark education law is shutting down schools', *BBC World News*, 6 March 2014. http://www.bbc.com/news/world-asia-india-26333713 (Accessed 9 July 2014)
7. '54 school headmasters suspended in Bihar for misusing SSA funds', *Zee News*, 23 June 2014. http://zeenews.india.com/news/bihar/54-school-headmasters-suspended-in-bihar-for-misusing-funds_942028.html (Accessed 9 July 2014)
8. 'Up to 20,000 teachers in Bihar hired on forged degrees', *Indian Express*, 3 July 2014. http://indianexpress.com/article/india/india-others/up-to-20000-teachers-in-bihar-hired-on-forged-degrees/ (Accessed 9 July 2014)
9. Gohain, Manash Pratim. '99% fail test for school teachers', *Times of India*, 2 Jan 2013. http://timesofindia.indiatimes.com/home/education/news/99-fail-test-for-school-teachers/articleshow/17848944.cms (Accessed 9 July 2014)
10. Nanda, Prashant K. 'Aspirations bring girls to schools, lack of toilets drives them away', *Livemint.com*, 19 June 2014. http://www.livemint.com/Politics/XgN1XAJgwljqQ42NNlGRQM/Aspirations-bring-girls-to-schools-lack-of-toilets-drives-t.html (Accessed 9 July 2014)

11. Tuli, Aanchal. 'Banning sex education is not a solution', *Times of India*, 7 July 2014. http://timesofindia.indiatimes.com/life-style/relationships/parenting/Banning-sex-education-is-not-a-solution/articleshow/37900966.cms (Accessed 9 July 2014)
12. Rohatgi, Meenakshi. '30% girls in Maharashtra are child brides', *Times of India*, 6 July 2014. http://timesofindia.indiatimes.com/city/pune/30-girls-in-Maharashtra-are-child-brides-Study/articleshow/37870524.cms (Accessed 9 July 2014)
13. Bhowmick, Nilanjana. 'More Children Are Going to School in India, but They're Learning Less', *Time*, 8 July 2014. http://time.com/2956888/india-education-decline-world-bank-report/ (Accessed 10 July 2014)

A NOTE ON THE AUTHORS

Kovid Gupta is pursuing an MBA from Cornell University. He holds a BBA, BS, and BA from the University of Texas at Austin. He has previously worked on Teach For India's alumni impact team. As a screenwriter, he has written for popular television shows *Balika Vadhu*, *Bade Achhe Lagte Hain*, and *Chhan Chhan*.

Shaheen Mistri is the Founder of Akanksha, and the Founder and CEO of Teach For India. She has served as an advisor and board member to other organizations, including the Latika Roy Foundation, Ummeed, The Indian School Leadership Institute, Akanksha, Teach For All, and the Government of India.